HAND HIM OVER
TO THE ENEMY

HAND HIM OVER TO THE ENEMY
HOW DOES A MOMMA DO THAT?

*A 31 Day Devotional to Encourage You That Light
Can Break Through the Darkness*

KRISAN MARKESE

Xulon Press

Xulon Press
2301 Lucien Way #415
Maitland, FL 32751
407.339.4217
www.xulonpress.com

Unless otherwise indicated, Scripture quotations taken from the Holy Bible, New International Version (NIV). Copyright © 1973, 1978, 1984, 2011 by Biblica, Inc.™. Used by permission. All rights reserved.

Scripture quotations taken from the King James Version (KJV) – *public domain.*

Scripture quotations taken from the English Standard Version (ESV). Copyright © 2001 by Crossway, a publishing ministry of Good News Publishers. Used by permission. All rights reserved.

Scripture quotations taken from the New American Standard Bible (NASB). Copyright © 1960, 1962, 1963, 1968, 1971, 1972, 1973, 1975, 1977, 1995 by The Lockman Foundation. Used by permission. All rights reserved.

Scripture quotations taken from the Holy Bible, New Living Translation (NLT). Copyright ©1996, 2004, 2007 by Tyndale House Foundation. Used by permission of Tyndale House Publishers, Inc.

Scripture quotations taken from the New King James Version (NKJV). Copyright © 1982 by Thomas Nelson, Inc. Used by permission. All rights reserved.

Scripture quotations taken from the Bible in Basic English (BBE) – *public domain.*

Scripture quotations taken from The Holy Bible, English Standard Version Copyright © 2001 by Crossway Bibles, a division of Good News Publishers.

Scripture quotations taken from the Young's Literal Translation (YLT)) – public domain.

 <a href="https://pngtree.com/free-backgrounds">free background photos from pngtree.com</a>

Printed in the United States of America.

ISBN-13: 978-1-6322-1687-8

DEDICATION

I dedicated this book to all those wonderful friends that I have leaned on throughout the years. Those whose lives have either been impacted by the poor choices of others or who have the gift of discernment and wisdom. Those who have "held up" my family through this time, but also who I have been honored to "hold up". Because of you, I am determined to help others make it through similar times in their lives, by presenting these words of encouragement from someone who's come along side others, as well as experienced those moments themselves.

There are many of you, but I must mention those who have impacted me the most (in alphabetical order, as to not put one above the other). Cathy Rogman Ballard, Cyndi Block, Cathy Gregory, Elizabeth Hackbarth, Alexia Remus, Joyce Salfisberg, Michelle Trammell. I LOVE AND APPRECIATE EACH AND EVERYONE OF YOU, YOU ARE PRICELESS AND IRREPLACEABLE!!

CONTENTS

ACKNOWLEDGMENTS

I first and foremost want to thank my precious Heavenly Father for trusting me with such an endeavor! He is so gracious and kind to use such a broken vessel!

I want to thank my wonderful husband, Pastor Ron Markese, for putting up with all the long hours of absenteeism, while I plugged away at transforming my vocabulary into words on paper. He has been a great encouragement and moral support when I needed it most! Thanks, honey for your sense of humor that keeps me "light"! (I can tend to be on the serious side).

I would be remiss if I did not mention my children, Stephanie and Mychal. They are the inspiration behind this entire book. I love you with all my heart and wish you to have all of Jesus you can handle! I hope you don't feel "overexposed" here. I want to thank you for allowing me to share our family's journey at a bit of your expense, so maybe others can be encouraged and blessed.

Thank you, Aiden and Ryan, for being the best grandsons a "Nani" could have! YOU ARE BOTH AMAZING!!

I thank my Mom (Ruth Eucker) and Dad (Roger Eucker, now passed), for raising me with a great "moral compass" that eventually led to our salvation! You were a great example to each of us of how to love others around us.

I want to thank our friend Dr. Jeff Rebarcak! He is the one who relentlessly stayed on me to start writing and keep writing! Thank you, Dr. Jeff, for making me believe I could actually do this, when I was sure that I could not! (I heard your voice in my head many times through this experience). You are a blessing to SOOOOOOO many people, and I know that there are hundreds, if not thousands, out there who wish they had this same opportunity to thank you publicly for your help "chiropractically," spiritually, and emotionally. You are the best encourager I know!!!

A special "Thank you!!" goes to our amazing niece Elisabeth Lively, who agreed to take on the daunting job of editing even before she knew how inept her aunt Krisan was. Thank you, Elisabeth, for making this devotional more enjoyable to read and for giving me a lesson in the proper way to present the book (even though I didn't listen to everything)! Thank you for all the hours you put in and the patience you showed during this time! I LOVE YOU!!!!

Last, but not least, I want to thank all my prayer partners, who have prayed for us during this season of our lives and while I wrote this book. I will not mention you by name because there are so many, and I do not want to miss anyone. You know who you are!!! I love you all so very much and thank you for all the encouraging words and support you have given Ron and I! I really believe we could not have made it through all this without you!!

INTRODUCTION

B reaking the seal to open a notebook and begin writing has never been a difficult task, until now. This notebook was different, probably the most expensive I've ever bought, $10, Woohoo! Beautifully embossed with flowers and teal blue. So, what is so difficult? Well, about four weeks ago the Lord woke me up with this thought "hand him over to the enemy" (speaking of our son, who was currently making some very bad decisions for his life), what? Then later told me, "write about it". That's what's so difficult! I've never written anything, as far as publishing, and furthermore, I never had a desire to write anything! I was never the greatest student; my teachers would attest to that! I never paid enough attention to how to write anything or even construct a proper sentence, sorry Miss McGowen, I know you tried!!! So, to take on the challenge of writing a book is overwhelming to say the least.

Besides not paying attention in school I also had an opportunity about a year-and-a-half ago to learn more about writing a book. I was attending classes to be ordained, while we were there someone came in from outside and said "we just saw a cloud in the shape of a quill just sitting on the top of this building". Then there was a prophecy given, that there would be many writers come from the school. Well, I sat there and thought "not me I don't have any interest in writing a book!!!"

They had classes that we sat through to instruct us how to write a book. I did listen, and actually thought it was quite interesting, but the entire time I was thinking about my friend who was thinking about writing a book, I even texted her to tell her about the person who was speaking and that she should look into getting her book. The joke's on me! God has such a great sense of humor I can just see Him with a grin on His glorious face and shaking His head saying "Oh Krisan, if you only realized what is coming". Then, 14.5 months later, we were going through a rough patch with our son. Up until this time God had most always spoken to us about just showing mercy. MERCY?? He doesn't need mercy; he needs a good kick in the pants!!! BUT GOD'S WAYS ARE NOT OUR OWN!! So, we showed mercy, to the point that we were accused by many of being "enablers". Oh, I hate that label!!! (but I digress).

This was a different time; it was time to "hand him over to the enemy". The Lord had spoken to both my husband and myself about this. He gave each of us different scriptures about the same thing, at the same time. We were overwhelmed with emotion by the thought!! We each had not told the other yet and our emotions were at "full tilt". Then one morning I shared with my husband the thing I felt the Lord was saying to me. To my surprise the Lord had spoken to him about the same thing as well.

> "When they sin against You—for there is no one who
> does not sin—
> and You become angry with them and give them over to
> the enemy,
> who takes them captive to a land far away or near;"
> **2 Chronicles 6:36** NIV
> (my emphasis added)

> *"Furthermore, just as they did not think it worthwhile to*
> *retain the knowledge of God,*
> *so God gave them over to a depraved mind, so that they*
> *do what ought not to be done.*
> *They have become filled with every kind of wickedness,*
> *evil, greed and depravity.*
> *They are full of envy, murder, strife, deceit and malice.*
> *They are gossips, slanderers, God-haters, insolent,*
> *arrogant and boastful;*
> *they invent ways of doing evil; they disobey their parents;*
> *they have no understanding, no fidelity, no love, no mercy.*
> *Although they know God's righteous decree that those*
> *who do such things deserve death,*
> *they not only continue to do these very things but also*
> *approve of those who practice them."*
> **Romans 1:28**

This is also God's mercy, whether it looks that way to you or not! He has it in His control, the enemy will not be able to do anything to them without God's permission. But on the other hand, they do open themselves up to more attacks, because of their choices.

After the initial shock of this, we proceeded to do what God instructed us to do. We kicked him out, waking the next day to this confirmation of

> *"Drive out the mocker, and out goes strife; quarrels and*
> *insults are ended."*
> **Proverbs 22:10** NIV

Now, the thing about our son (and daughter), they have never been children that "outwardly mock, or quarrel". They have always come across "on the outside" to respect us and to honor us. However, what they do on the outside does not always reflect what's on the inside. Afterall, "actions speak louder than words", right?!

When we finally got to a place where we felt comfortable sharing with others what was going on, "the rest of the story" began to unfold. I was sharing with a friend that God told us to "Hand him over to the enemy", I then said to her "how does a momma do that?". At that moment God spoke to my heart "I want you to write about it". In the weeks following He began to give me conformation after confirmation. Every conference or prophetic outsider that I met would prophetically say "You're going to write a book!". My response was always "well, I guess I am", but this was VERY OVERWHELMING to me, and I had no idea how this would actually happen.

One thing that I want to mention before I "cast this boat off", this process has taken several years, so these children of ours do not necessarily look the same today as they did when the particular "days" were written. I wish I could say that things are perfect and have all turned out to be a "happy ending". It has not YET, but my promise from my Father is, that it will!!!

I have prayed my way through this and we'll see where it ends up! I also wanted to share the many songs the Lord used to minister to me as we went through our journey, please take time to listen to them each day, along with the devotional. Maybe they will cause you to "break out" of your thoughts and into His, as they did me. I hope you enjoy hearing about our journey and most of all I hope this will be a book that encourages you, gives you hope and draws you closer to our precious Lord!

Blessings!! ~ *Krisan*

Day 1

Garbage Fire

Ultimately handing your son or daughter (or spouse, or grandchild or niece or nephew or whoever) over to the enemy is the same as when The Lord asked Abraham to sacrifice his son, his only son on the altar. When the God of the universe, the King of all kings asks you to give up your loved one you have to know that you can trust Him with them. We must know that His plan and His purposes will go forward just as the plans for Isaac went forward. We have to believe that the same God who gave Angels charge over Isaac to say *"Do not lay a hand on the boy"* will do the same for our loved one.

> *"Do not lay a hand on the boy"*
> **Genesis 22: 9-12** *NIV*

Handing them over feels like you're letting them drowned, so hard to watch your loved one suffer so. But God has a plan, and right now it looks like that plan includes suffering, that plan includes coming to the end of themselves, that plan includes being backed up in a corner, that plan includes not knowing what to do and coming to a place where you realize if you don't depend on Christ nothing will change.

"But as I told you, you have seen me and still you do not believe. All those the Father gives me will come to me, and whoever comes to me I will never drive away.
For I have come down from heaven not to do my will but to do the will of Him who sent me.
And this is the will of Him who sent me, that I shall lose none of all those He has given me, but raise them up at the last day.
For my Father's will is that everyone who looks to the Son and believes in Him shall have eternal life, and I will raise them up at the last day."
John 6:36-40 NIV
(my emphasis added)

I have not been handling this transition very well, I have been angry with God and angry with my son, and angry with everyone that I have thought should have tried to help him and did not. I feel like I am in the fire and I just want out, NOW!!!! When you're in the fire long enough eventually the garbage comes out, and the Lord is there to scrape the dross off.

It's hard to put into words the feelings that you have when you're going through the fire. Have you ever smelled a fire that's full of garbage? That's how I have felt this week.

"For we are to God the pleasing aroma of Christ among those who are being saved and those who are perishing".
II Corinthians 2:15 NIV

I haven't felt like I was a pleasing aroma this week, as I was in the fire the dross came to the top, the ugliness and attitudes, the scoffing and sarcasm comes up, I definitely feel like the garbage fire. But you know what? GOD WAS STANDING THERE IN THE FIRE WITH ME, JUST LIKE THE HEBREW SONS!!! He was there comforting me, even when I didn't realize it, or deserve it.

*God allows us to be in the fire so that we will be purified.
So that we can become what II Corinthians 2:15 said, "the
pleasing aroma of Christ" ... "AMONG THOSE WHO ARE
BEING SAVED AND THOSE WHO ARE PERISHING"*
(my emphasis added)

More times than not, when we hear the above scripture mentioned, we only hear part a, not part b. May I bring part b to your attention?

When we are a pleasing aroma it's for the "lost" around us, not just to be a pleasing aroma to God alone, but when our aroma draws men unto Himself, that is what makes that aroma pleasing to God.

Oh, how I want to please God! That is to do as we are all commissioned to do, "draw all men unto Him", (that includes women and children BTW).

Going through the fire is not easy, and one thing I know for sure is that I don't want to have to keep going through the fire for the same reasons. So, whether I am pushed in by the force of others or by my own short comings, I know that, if while I'm in it, I can trust in Christ my Savior to bring me through it. I will come out not even smelling like smoke, but will have become a pleasing aroma of Christ.

I know...

*"that all things work together for good to them
that love God,
to them who are called according to his purpose"*
Romans 8:28 KJV

and I will come out as pure gold as well as my family
with me!!!!!

Is there any area of "stench" you need to pray about?
You can substitute my "areas" for yours
In the following prayer

Heavenly Father,

I must repent for my actions and "goings on" of this week. I know that this is not how You wish for me to respond and that You do not deserve any of the "mouthieness" I gave You this week. Please forgive me of every sin and cleanse me from all unrighteousness. I declare today that I will trust You to repair the broken hearts involved in "all this". I will lean not on my understanding, but on Yours. I will try to respond in a more dignified and pleasing way as we proceed through this process. Thank You for Your love for me, that You will never give up on me, that You are with me and that I can trust in You.

In Jesus Name
AMEN

Suggested Song: "How Deep The Father's Love" by Liberty Campus Band"

DAY 2

THE ROLLERCOASTER RIDE

As I'm writing today our nation is in turmoil over presidential elections, and my heart is in turmoil over my son having to go through disappointment after disappointment. It's heart wrenching, in both cases. To watch our nation become so divided and to watch your loved one be disappointed, even though you know they brought this upon themselves. At the same time, it gives me peace to know that God is in control. He's in control of our nation, even when we don't understand what He's doing. And He's in control of our loved one, even when He has asked us to hand them over to the enemy.

It is not an easy task to say the least, it's heart-breaking, it's emotional, it's a rollercoaster, AND IT'S EXHAUSTING! There are tears and there are times of joy. When you know that God is in control you can be assured that He will keep us in perfect peace!!!

"You keep him in perfect peace whose mind is stayed on You, because he trusts in You."
Isaiah 26:3 ESV
(my emphasis added)

This rollercoaster is not the most enjoyable one I've ever been on. I guess the reference to the roller coasters is because I was just on one a few days ago, and it was exciting. The ups and downs, the winding turns, the darkness and not knowing whether you're going to be going up, or slowing down, or if you will be sprayed with water unexpectedly. The difference is those kinds of roller coasters are fun and adventurous, the kind we are on definitely IS NOT!

With our loved one's disappointments come the irrational excuses for why they've done what they've done. How do you listen to ungodly reasoning for actions? How do you respond? In our case we VERY LOVINGLY state our case why this is not what God would want, then we shut up and pray.

Jesus ALWAYS spoke lovingly and so should we! The only reference to Jesus even coming close to sounding angry was when he "cleansed the Temple"...It was unacceptable for His Father's House to be unclean! It is interesting as you read about "the cleansing of the temple" in Matthew 21, that it only spans two verse, 12 & 13. Then Jesus goes back to healing the sick. Looks to me that Jesus spent less time talking about the sin and more time tending to the sinners He loved so much. Can you try that??

On this journey we're walking through we will experience many "roller coaster" moments. If you would ask someone how to keep from getting dizzy on a roller coaster, or any other moving ride, they would tell you to "keep your eyes on a fixed point". So, on this ride we must keep our eyes fixed on Christ.

> *"... fixing our eyes on Jesus,*
> *the author and perfecter of **our faith**..."*
> ***Hebrews 12:2a*** *NASB*

I am reminded of one of my favorite songs as a young Christian, "Perfect Peace", it reminds us of Gods promise to keep us in His peace, even with the confusion that tries to take us out. As we focus on Him instead of the circumstances around us, He will keep us in His Peace and perfect our faith!!

Try talking to The Lord about how you've lost your focus

Lord,

I am exhausted today! I am asking today that You will allow me to crawl up into Your ever-loving arms and just let me rest in You. Thank you so much for the love and mercy You give to us each day. Help me to keep my eyes fixed on You, that my faith might be perfected, and that I might not grow dizzy on these roller coaster days of our lives. I ask for Your grace to sustain me and cause me to reflect Your loving ways.

In Jesus Name
AMEN

Suggested Song: "Perfect Peace/My Peace I Leave With You" by Andrae' Crouch & the Disciples (on "this is another Day" album)

DAY 3

GET OUT OF THE WAY

"In their hearts humans plan their course, but the Lord establishes their steps."
Proverbs 16:9 NIV

"Whoever gives heed to instruction prospers, and blessed is the one who trusts in the Lord."
Proverbs 16:20 NIV

How come when we know we are doing what God wants us to do, it's so difficult to continue to walk it out? God told us to hand our son over to the enemy, but what we want to do is to rescue him.

Just think about this for a minute "hand him over to the enemy". How do I pray then, do I pray for protection? do I pray for guidance? do I pray for peace? IDK, I think what I should do is just pray God's will be done. That's it!

It is not easy to watch your loved one walk in the ways of the world, it's not easy to see them overwhelmed with their life circumstances. As a parent all you want to do is rescue, all you want to do is protect, all you want to do is make sure that they're okay.

But, in this situation, that's not what God wants us to do. God wants us to trust Him, He wants us to thank Him for working in their lives, even when we don't see that work being accomplished or even started. He wants us to trust in His love for them, He wants us to trust that He has everything under control, even when it may not look that way, AT ALL!

So today I choose to be thankful, today I choose to trust in my God that supplies all my needs and the needs of my children according to His riches in Glory.

> *"But my God shall supply all your need according to His riches in glory by Christ Jesus."*
> **Philippians 4:19** *KJV*
> *(my emphasis added)*

WOW, that verse just "struck" me! The part that was "highlighted" to me today was "according to His riches in glory" – as I understand this portion of the verse, after looking up in the Greek word studies, it is the same as saying "according to what Christ is worth". In other words, All my needs are supplied based on Christs worth"

WOOHOO!!! I'll claim that!

> *"The decrees of the Lord are firm,*
> *and all of them are righteous.*
> *They are more precious than gold,*
> *than much pure gold;*
> *they are sweeter than honey,*
> *than honey from the honeycomb."*
> **Psalms 19:9b-10** *NIV*

If the Lords decrees are more precious than gold, how much more is He, Himself?! Our supply is endless! Our supply is beyond what we can fathom! Thank You Jesus that in You is our supply!

So again, I choose to ... thank him for being our supply. I choose to thank Him for what He's doing in my loved one's lives, I choose to thank Him for the love that He surrounds them with, I choose to thank Him for His goodness and His grace and for penetrating their hearts with His love. I choose to thank Him for the Divine appointments that He has already planned for them, and I choose to not get in His way today.

This is a daily decision and I'm going to discuss with the Lord. But I know He understands my heart and my intentions. I choose this day not to get in His way, and hopefully tomorrow I won't get in His way either!

Try confessing to God how you might be getting in His way

Jesus,

I raise my hands in praise to You today as I think about all that You have, can and will accomplish. Help me to be more like You. Help me to be of great worth, as You are! Help me to stay out of Your way and allow You to work in _____ life. Thank You for everything You are accomplishing, even if I don't see it. Thank You that in You is my supply! May Your time frame go forth and mine be thrown out. I will trust in You today and forever more!! I love You Jesus!!

AMEN

Suggested Song: "Be Still and Know" by Newsong

11

DAY 4

FORMLESS AND VOID

Going from one addiction to another (these can be people as well as narcotics). That's what it "looks like" as we watch our kids live their adult lives. "addictions" are not only "drugs", it can be people as well, and what I mean by that is, we as individuals can be drawn to people as our "addiction".

I once had a friend that I depended on solely to speak God's words to me. I trusted everything she said. I WAS ADDICTED!! God had used her in tremendous ways to draw me closer to Himself. But then God decided to move her out of my life. At the moment, I was devastated to say the least. But God used that situation to draw me unto Himself and assured me He could speak to me personally, not just through her. The VERY sad part to that story is that after she moved away from me, she also moved away from the Lord. It is a perfect example of how we really don't know someone's heart, only God does!!

That addiction, unbeknownst to me, was actually putting more space between the Lord and myself, because I was replacing Holy Spirit with this friend.

Getting back to my children... They can't be happy with their lives! They both seem sad and just have no direction. Yet we're the weird Bible believing parents who have the audacity to think that Christ should be Lord over everything.

Now I do believe that our kids (do you know what kids are? A frolicking animal who butts up against things for no reason – maybe we ought to change our term to... children! After all *"Death and life are in the power of the tongue..." Prov. 18:21 ESV*), I mean our CHILDREN, do know some foundational truths that will always "be there" after all *"God's word does not return void" (reference to Isaiah 55:11 NIV)*, but at this juncture I don't see it.

So, what do I believe? I believe the enemy wants to take them out of the picture (NOT ON MY WATCH), I believe that our God is bringing them to the end of themselves! I believe that there will be a day when those two children we raised to live for Christ WILL LIVE FOR CHRIST!! I also believe they will be leaders for Christ!!! That's what I believe!!! Because that is what I have prayed for all their sweet little lives!!!! I serve a God who "calls those things that are not as though they were" AND "who brings dead bones to life" woohoooooooo!!! GLORY TO GOD!!!!

My hope is in Christ! I cannot be distracted or discouraged by the schemes of the enemy, because that would mean that I have allowed the enemy to steal my joy, and also that I am once again falling into unbelief. This is something we have to be on guard to recognize, as soon as the emotions prick at us, before we would allow them to overtake us.

> *"In the beginning God created the heavens and the earth.*
> *Now the earth was formless and empty,*
> *darkness was over the surface of the deep,*
> *and the Spirit of God was hovering over the waters."*
> **Genesis 1:1**

This is another favorite verse of mine (I have a lot!). My perspective of our children's spiritual lives is "formless, empty and dark". I have a VERY difficult time accepting that, AS I SHOULD!! And this verse has given me a sweet peace, knowing that Holy Spirit hovers over what is deep within them. It also gives me such an enormous amount of anticipation for what the Lord can

14

transform their lives to be. This is a verse that inspired me to pray the following prayer over my children. I invite you to pray it over your "loved one", whether child, spouse, niece, nephew, husband or wife, etc.

Do you have an "addiction" that needs to be broken?
Talk to God about that then pray the following prayer

Dear Holy Spirit,

I ask You to please hover over _____
_____, over their formless and empty spiritual lives. I ask that You would allow him/her to feel Your presence and love for them. I ask that You would mold and make _____ into the woman/man of God that You have always intended them to be. Help me to see them the way You see them and be content that their lives may look different than mine. Thank You for the peace and grace You are giving me to walk through this journey. I LOVE YOU SO MUCH!!!

In Jesus Name
AMEN

Suggested song: "What A Wonderful Savior" by Newsong

Bonus song: "Graves to Gardens" by Evelation Worship

DAY 5

NO DADDY NO

*"TRUST IN THE LORD WITH ALL YOUR HEART AND LEAN
NOT ON YOUR OWN UNDERSTANDING;
in all your ways submit to Him,
and He will make your paths straight."*
Proverbs 3:5&6 *NIV*
(my emphasis added)

This is my husband's life scripture. A scripture that I have heard so many times and one that brings encouragement. BUT there are days, like today, when I want to shout "I HAVE, AND I STILL DON'T FEEL DIRECTED!!"

Isn't it difficult not to LEAN ON OUR OWN UNDERSTANDING?! There is another "key" word in this scripture though, it is the word "submit". I CAN HEAR YOU!!! "Now you've gone and crossed the line Krisan, do not use that word!" In our 21st century mind-sets using the word "submit" conjures up all sorts of "trust" issues. We have been inundated with the worlds point of view that we must not "bow" or "submit" to anyone or anything. Because this will surely lead to us becoming their servant and being "less than". I think you understand what I am speaking of!

Well, thank God we do not live according to this world, but according to Christ Jesus our Lord! We must "submit" "**all our ways**" to the Lord. Our emotions, our ideas (that usually are contrary to His), our way of doing things, etc. We must exchange our ways for "The Way".

Another scripture that is "ringing in my ears" tonight is "The joy of the Lord is your strength" BOY OH BOY...I don't feel joyful! I WOULD IF MY KIDS WERE SERVING GOD WITH ALL THEIR HEARTS!!!! BUT THEY ARE NOT!!! Oh, how my heart aches.... how sad I feel!!! Will I ever not have this sadness? I don't see an end to it!! What can I say? That's just where I am right now!!

A few years back I was asking the Lord about the next scripture ...

> *"This Day is holy to our Lord. Do not grieve,*
> *for the joy of the Lord is your strength."*
> **Nehemiah 8:10** NIV

I was discussing with the Lord about how this scripture explains where our strength comes from, but I didn't understand where the joy came from. He shared with me a vision of my son, who has two young boys. In the vision, he was pushing his youngest son through darkness and the older son was hanging on his arm saying "no daddy no, no daddy no, he's going to be scared he'll get hurt", but my son kept pushing him through the darkness. What the Lord showed me was that my son knew what was on the other side he would not stop pushing because he knew that there was light and safety on the other side, but his older son did not know that. The Lord told me "that's when you find my joy, when you can stop hanging on my arms, trying to stop me, and just trust me". Today is just one of those days I need to trust, and I know, because the Lord told me I can, I can find Joy in doing it!!

Talk to God about your "tough" questions
And what you tend to not trust Him with

Heavenly Father,

You are holy and worthy of all praise! I thank You for always being willing to answer our questions. You are just, kind and true. Thank You that we can trust Your voice and lean on You! Help me today to not lean on my own understanding, but submit my feelings and emotions to You, so that I may receive joy in the process and then have Your strength to make it through this journey.

In Jesus Name
AMEN

Song suggestion: "Through It All" by Andrae' Crouch (lyric video)

DAY 6

DO YOU BELIEVE?

This is a question that comes up often in my mind but not a question for someone else, a question for myself. I question, do I believe all the time but then the next question comes do I trust? Sometimes I just don't know the answer to that question. I would love to say yes, I believe, yes, I trust! But in all reality, it's not always the case and I find myself constantly saying Lord, help my unbelief, please help my unbelief!

I absolutely love the song "We Believe" and I do! I do believe in God the Father, I do believe in God the Son, I do believe in the Holy Spirit and that they are three and one, I do believe! BUT when it comes to my kids sometimes, I don't know what to think. How did they get here? how did they get to this place in life? how did we get to a place where my dreams have not become a reality?

I always dreamed of talking to my kids about the things of God, the dreams that the Lord had given them, their visions, their hopes for the future, their ministries. Those are my dreams, to have a relationship with my kids so centered around Christ and the things of Christ.

But instead I have to constrain myself from sharing all the things of the Lord I want to share, because they won't receive it or they honestly just don't have a clue what I'm talking about.

Do I believe? And do I believe that God can turn this around? Do I believe my children will choose Christ over the things of this world? Will they? Will they before I die?

All these questions are valid questions, but when I look at all of them, I am aware that I am surely focusing on the wrong things. This cannot be how God intended me to live my life

So, what to do?

> *"Finally, brethren,*
> *whatsoever things are true,*
> *whatsoever things are honest,*
> *whatsoever things are just,*
> *whatsoever things are pure,*
> *whatsoever things are lovely,*
> *whatsoever things are of good report;*
> *if there be any virtue,*
> *and if there be any praise,*
> *think on these things."*
> ***Philippians 4:8*** *KJV*

I painted this scripture on my foyer wall in one of our homes... WHAT WAS I THINKING?? It took forever!! I can recall going up and down that 11 ft. ladder so many times, to check and make sure the writing was straight and each letter was in proper proportion with each other. WHAT A TASK!!! BUT it was worth all the effort and a wonderful daily reminder! Also, a perfect example of the effort it takes to keep Gods Word before us.

Sometimes it's just not easy. We read a scripture and think "oh that's good", "That's really good!", only to turn around and forget what we just read.

To plant God's Word in our heart we must continually go back to that scripture. Look at it, make sure WE line up with it. Make sure we follow it. Make sure we cause it to become a beautiful piece of our life. I've heard of some people setting an alarm on their phone – with the scripture attached (It's not a bad way to memorize scripture either. Just sayin!) to help them to keep it before them to help them think on the good things throughout their day.

YES!!! THAT'S IT!!! Think on the things of the Lord!!

In the past few years my husband and I have become more interested in the "Feasts of The Lord". These are the feasts, or days that the Lord instructed the Israelites to observe throughout each year. These feasts are not just for the Jewish community, these feasts are "The Lords" feasts, that means they were intended for all of us to observe. We are just now, becoming more aware of what the feasts represent, we have enjoyed learning and making ourselves aware of their importance. In the process of learning about the feasts, we have also collected a few Tallit's. These are Prayer Shawls that are worn to cover (usually a man's) head. In Old Testament times, they were to cover the head and served also as a reminder of the commandments of God. In New testament, God set things in a different order, when He sent his Son to accomplish the purpose of the laws, to bring freedom. So, in our (my husbands and mine) Gentile world that is just learning about this, we use the tallit to cover the head and eyes to help block out the distractions and concentrate on our prayers (we only use them once in a while), but they do help you to concentrate more. On each of these tallit's you will find 4 "tzitzit", made of twisted cords, on each corner of the tallit, a fringe that represents (to us) Gods statutes and promises.

"When you see the tassels, you will remember and obey
all the commands of the LORD
instead of following your own desires
and defiling yourselves, as you are prone to do."
Numbers 15:39 NLT

We use the tallit to help us remember. There are more promises and encouragements in Gods word than any book ever written, because it is The Word of God!!

What promises do you need to remind yourself of?
Write them down, set and alarm, do whatever it takes
To continue to remember them

Dear Lord,

I BELIEVE You are a great and Mighty God Who uses Your Word to sustain us and lead us into right thinking. Thank You so much for helping me today to think on the good things. Help me to recall this scripture every time I am tempted to fall into one of my pity parties. Help me to remember all Your promises in Your word, and to live by Your statutes daily. Help me to trust You and give You praise continually, because You are Worthy of All Praise!!

In Jesus Name
AMEN

Suggested song: "We Believe" by Newsboys

DAY 7

DECREE AND DECLARE

In our lives we are faced with many questions ...where do I go? what do I do? who do I talk to? is this my responsibility?

Several times in the Word you will find that the people that courageously went forward in doing God's will first spend time in the wilderness, or in a place of solitude. These times were not usually times of rest and feasting, but they were times that the Lord spoke to these different individuals and gave them specific instructions.

If we want to possess spiritual power in our lives then we must first seek God's face, we must first spend time at his feet, and the more we do that the better we become at seeing, hearing and doing.

The key to any spiritual success is "doing what you see the Father doing"...If this is what Jesus did then how much more should we?!

In Romans 4:17 it says that Abraham served a God who brings life from death and calls those things that are not as though they were. Then we read in Ezekiel...

> *"He asked me, "Son of man, can these bones live?"*
> *I said, "Sovereign Lord, You alone know."*
> *Then He said to me, "Prophesy to these bones*
> *and say to them,*
> *'Dry bones, hear the word of the Lord!"*
> **Ezekiel 37:3**
> *(my emphasis added)*

Chapter 37 of Ezekiel is worth your time, to encourage you if not fill you with POWER!

We serve a God who from the beginning "Spoke", we must follow what we see our Father doing, this is a very good place to start. Paul tells us that our Father brings life from death and He also calls those things that are not as though they were. We have to walk courageously in this life and we have to begin to call the things that we know are God's will into existence. We must be the ones that decree and declare God's will. We must be the ones to speak life into those dead things in our lives and in our family's lives. WE must be the voice of heaven here on this earth, and what better way to do that than to speak what our Father is speaking over these awful situations!!

He speaks life not death! He speaks...

	NOT...
Blessings	Shame
Love	Condemnation
Joy	Death
Peace	Curses
Patience	Sarcasm
Mercy	HatredLies
Grace	Strife
Healing	Retaliation
Forgiveness	Defensive Speech
Endurance	Offensive Speech
Kindness	Insults
Truth	Judgments
	Assumptions

He speaks life and so should we!!

Keep a tally of the type of words you speak. Really!!!
It will help you see where your heart is
And where it could be
Not as an exercise to condemn,
But as one to strengthen your life in Him!!!

Heavenly Father,

I want to bring You Glory in every way, including my words and actions. I want to follow in Your footsteps, I want to do what I see You doing! I ask for Your help today to become bold and courageous. To speak those things into existence that the enemy wants obliterated. Help me today to be very aware of what I say and how those words influence me and those around me. Thank You for giving me another piece of your Rock to place my foot on today! Help me to be faithful to continue to follow Your path.

In Jesus Name
AMEN

Suggested song: "Come Alive (Dry Bones)" featuring Lauren Daigle on CentricWorship

DAY 8

FRAGRANCE OF THE LORD

When the Lord told me I was going to write a book, besides the fact of being shocked, I knew it was not going to be the easiest ride. I sensed that it was going to be just as much of a learning experience for me as for the future readers of the book. The title of the book refers to our son, but the context of the book is about our children, both of our children!

I just have the hardest time wrapping my brain around my children choosing the world over God. This week I thought about it so much and I've come to the conclusion "that you are who you hang out with!" And there's no getting around it! No matter who you choose to hang around with or who your children choose, more than likely we or they will end up taking on more of their traits than they take on of ours, especially if it's an exchange for good to bad.

I would love to say that my children have had some influence on their friends more than their friends have influenced them, but I don't think that's the truth. I do believe my children have influenced people for Christ, I can't deny them that! I know that they have talked to their friends about the Lord in the past, but I question whether they're doing it anymore. **But this could be all part of my clouded perspective!**

*"Now we see things imperfectly,
like puzzling reflections in a mirror,
but then we will see everything with perfect clarity.
All that I know now is partial and incomplete,
but then I will know everything completely,
just as God now knows me completely."*
1 Corinthians 13:12 NLT

And my plan is for this scripture to be the verse of our lives together...

*"But thanks be to God, who in Christ always leads us in triumphal procession,
and through us spreads the fragrance of the knowledge of him everywhere."*
2 Corinthians 2:14 ESV

Oh, how I want my family and myself to be a wonderful fragrance of the knowledge of Him everywhere!

I am very sensitive to fragrances myself. I am the only one that can choose what cologne my husband wears, because if it has an ingredient that "I can't handle" then it would be a waste of money, and cologne is not cheap. At least not the ones I can actually enjoy.

I don't want any "ingredient" in me to be offensive to anyone around me, and especially to the Lord. I want to be a pleasing aroma in His nostrils. I want to experience triumphal procession of my entire family living the way God has always intended! I am claiming that one!!!

Thanks be to God, In Christ This Can Happen!!!!

Do you have a scripture for your family?
Ask God to help you find one

Dear Abba,

I love You so much and am so thankful that You have a plan in the midst of every mess. I thank You that as I read Your Word, I am encouraged and ready for yet another day. Thank You that one day we will have a triumphal procession together with _____ _____. Bless my day Lord, and help me to spread the fragrance of the knowledge of You everywhere I go.

In Jesus Name
AMEN

Suggested Song: "You Are I AM" by MercyMe

DAY 9

GOD KNOWS

Years ago, a friend spoke this verse over my husband and I...

> *"because you have done this and have not*
> *withheld your son, your only son,*
> *I will surely bless you and make your descendants*
> *as numerous as the stars in the sky*
> *and as the sand on the seashore."*
> **Genesis 22:15-18** NIV

At that time, I don't remember seeing the phrase "because you have not withheld your son", probably because at that time I had not! Or maybe we thought we had, but today that phrase means something different then what it meant then.

As I read this scripture today, I see it in a totally different light. See God knows everything about us, He knows before we even do something, that we're going to do it, or not do it. We seem to always think in terms of the now, but He sees yesterday, He sees tomorrow and the now.

If we will only be obedient, He will bless us. As you know the Lord asked us to give our son over to the enemy, but at the time this verse was spoken over us we had not done that. *The Lord knows*, The Lord knows, **The Lord knows** what we're going to do.

He knows the steps were going to take, He knows the decisions that we will make, He knows our heart, He knows our thoughts, He knows what's going on around us and WE can know... when we're obedient, HE will bless us.

As I write today's devotional, I am enjoying our son and his boys like I never imagined 6 years ago. YES, IT HAS BEEN 6 YEARS THAT OUR SON IS CLEAN FROM DRUGS. At that time, I never thought this day would ever get here! But it has and WE ARE BLESSED!! There is still a long way to go, BUT GOD!! We see progress continually, ITS NEVER AS FAST AS WE WANT TO SEE AND EXPERIENCE IT!! BUT IT IS PROGRESS!!

Years ago, I remember hearing several different speakers behind the pulpit, after describing horrible situations they, or a family member had experienced, say "I would not change a thing". I remember thinking "Oh come on? Are you kidding me? Of course, you would!!"

Well, I can't speak for those folks, but I still would have wanted to change things. BUT I now have a better understanding of that statement! It's because of what you are going through that draws you closer to the Lord, and teaches you things you would have never learned. So yes, If I could not have been as close to God, as I find myself today, without facing these daunting circumstances, then I would agree ... "I would not change a thing!"

Thank You God, for the progress!! Thank You God, for the blessings!! Thank You God for the agony of the experience, because otherwise I and my family would not be where we find ourselves today. Trusting You in ways we never would have before. Able to minister to those we would not have had anything to share with, if not for our circumstances. THANK YOU JESUS, FOR YOUR BLOOD THAT CLEANSES US, EVEN WHEN WE DON'T SEE THAT WE NEED IT!

A great example of this is: Our son had just been incarcerated, yet again. Ron and I were devastated, but it was Sunday morning and our responsibility was to minister during the prayer time at our church. We went forward to pray for people (at this church, people formed a line in the isle, and came up one by one, and you prayed with which ever prayer team was available). Every person or couple that "happened" to come to us from the line asked "would you pray for our son; he is in jail?" WOW! I think it happened 3 or 4 times during that short prayer segment. As you can imagine, we were more than prepared to minister to these precious people! And not only were we able to pray from a place of experience, but with compassion as well. Afterwards, we sat back down blessed and blessing God!!

Our Father had made sure that not only did He capture the attention of those sent to us, but He captured ours as well.

Look for ways this week
Where God is trying to capture your attention

Dear Abba Father,

Thank you for not withholding Your Son. Thank You for being the best example of sacrificial love and compassion for us! Thank You that You are Jehovah El Roi, the God who sees me! You are so faithful to guide us, with the help of Holy Spirit, and we are so grateful for Your unrelenting love. Help me to continually be willing to obey You, no matter what You ask, always remembering that You are the Keeper of the ultimate plan.

In Jesus Name
AMEN

Suggested Song: "Favorite Name" by Newsong (Newsong/ Your Favorite Name is Father album)

DAY 10

RESTORATION FROM DEVESTATION

I love to create! From the time I was a child I remember my favorite times in life were those times that I was allowed to create. I had an Aunt, that we would go spend time with periodically, she always had projects to work on. She also had different projects of her own that she was constantly working on. She used to do "Artex" paints, remember those? If you do, you are "getting up there" Ha! I digress! Anyway, I remember making caterpillars out of marbles, then we would put them in the oven and cause the marbles to crack on the inside to make them even more beautiful. We also made wonderful orange drinks from peppermint sticks and oranges. I think spending time with Aunt Dorothy fueled my need to create.

Our children will call me from time to time with requests of "How do I do_____? Or "can you fix this? Last year I renovated my daughters newly purchased townhome. That was fun! It went from a dark dingy cave-like dwelling, to a bright beautiful home for our daughter. Making something beautiful again is even more invigorating when you're spending someone else's money!!

In moments of creativity like that, I find myself asking for The Lords help, then He inspires in totally different ways then I ever expected. Or if I am needing strength that just is not there, and am by myself, I call on the Lord for His strength, and Voila! I have the strength of Samson. I love how we can find God in the middle of all we do!

One of my favorite past times, in my adult years, is restoring old furniture, actually anything old, into something new and fresh. I have restored several pieces of furniture, wood, metal, plastic, upholstered etc. You name it, I've probably restored it. I even made an already used child's red motorized car into a Black Batmobile! That was fun!! My point is, I enjoy watching anything that has been destroyed and devastated by life and make it new again! I love to create and make new!

In the same way I enjoy creating, I know that God enjoys creating! Afterall, it is the fifth word used in the Bible. It is the first action of God that we see in the Bible. We can see many times in His word that He is great at making things new, mainly people. He is always ready and willing to make us new again!

Today I am reminded of God's Great Grace and love for us!! We have a friend who is going through such a devastating time in his life, it's very hard to watch! I know he feels abandoned; I know that in those feelings he's making wrong choices. And that in that state of mind, he is still making the same choices that he was making before, that contributed to the situation he finds himself in now. He has not changed, because he didn't feel the ultimate mistake was his own. He is not "owning" any of it, and therefore it leaves him in a place of misery and continual unhappiness, as well as those in his family. But I'm reminded that whether we are a child, a teenager, an adult, or a senior adult... we still have to own our own choices.

We cannot blame the devastation that others have placed upon us in the past for the choices that we make right now. Our future depends on how we own our choices.

God's plan was never for us to wallow in the devastation of our lives. His plan has always been to help us rise up from the ashes and create a beautiful picture of grace, mercy and love in our lives.

It's up to you whether you allow the devastation that you've gone through to ruin the rest of your life OR to allow God to create a beautiful picture of restoration from the devastation.

> *He will ...*
> *"bestow on them a crown of beauty instead of ashes,*
> *the oil of joy instead of mourning,*
> *and a garment of praise instead of a spirit of despair.*
> *They will be called oaks of righteousness,*
> *a planting of the Lord for the display of his splendor."*
> **Isaiah 61:3** *NIV*
> *(my emphasis added)*

I want to be an OAK OF RIGHTEOUSNESS ... YES!! ... SO, JESUS CAN BE GLORIFIED!!!!

I want to be a "planting of the Lord", sometimes the Lord "plants" us in places that our "roots" are not used to, but He will help us become acclimated to where He has planted us. He will help us to flourish and become "oaks" (those are very strong trees!). But oaks take a long time to grow, so don't expect things to be "fast" in the acclimating process! You'll be stronger for it! Also, if you know anything about gardening, you know that "ashes" are a great source of nutrients. So not only does God plant us, but He uses the ashes of our lives to help us grow stronger. THEN we can become "displays of His splendor".

WOOHOO! GO GOD!!!

What are the choices you need to "own"?
Maybe have a conversation with God about those

Lord,

Thank You that Your plan for us is to have beauty for the ashes of our lives. What a wonderful promise for us to depend on! Thank You that as we are faithful to study Your Word, You are always faithful to give us encouragement and lead us into Truth. May I give all my ashes to You today. I am confident that You will turn them in to something beautiful that brings You Glory.

In Jesus Name
AMEN

Suggested song: "Beauty for Ashes" by Sean and Sean (Upstairs album)

DAY 11

HOPE DEFERRED

There are many of us "in the same boat", we have been faithful followers of Christ and we have been devastated by the actions of others. We find ourselves almost giving up on believing that anything will change. We have been here for so many years, that we no longer feel the hope we once felt concerning the mess, or our loved one. It is a very sad and frustrating place to find yourself! BUT GOD!!!

We must remember that "we struggle not against flesh and blood", we find ourselves in the midst of battles that we are frustrated in because we are trying to fight the people that seem to be creating the problem, we hold grudges against them, we are angry with them, maybe we find ourselves in the midst of unforgiveness, because they just don't stop. The key here is to not fight them, but to fight with Gods might against the "principalities of this dark world".

"For our struggle is not against flesh and blood, but against the rulers, against the authorities, against the powers of this dark world and against the spiritual forces of evil in the heavenly realms. Therefore put on the full armor of God, so that when the Day of evil comes, you may be able to stand your ground, and after you have done everything, to stand.

Stand firm then, with the belt of truth buckled around your waist, with the breastplate of righteousness in place, and with your feet fitted with the readiness that comes from the gospel of peace. In addition to all this, take up the shield of faith, with which you can extinguish all the flaming arrows of the evil one.
Take the helmet of salvation and the sword of the Spirit, which is the word of God. And pray in the Spirit on all occasions with all kinds of prayers and requests.
With this in mind, be alert and always keep on praying for all the Lord's people."
Ephesians 6:12

I am a table leader for a woman's bible study at our church. (not because I have such great wisdom, but because I have a great big mouth! Ha!) ANYWAY, in sharing with my table of ladies, I heard words come from my mouth I had never heard before, and I want to share those words with you today.

Our table discussion was focusing on Hope. We had been sharing segments of our different stories (we each have a story to tell) and we got on the subject of "hope differed"

"Hope deferred makes the heart sick,
but a longing fulfilled is a tree of life."
Proverbs 13:12 NIV

The question arose "how do we still have hope while we are waiting for the "longing to be fulfilled"? The answer The Lord gave me came from my recent experience, but I had never put it into words before...so to me it was profound (a profound word from God not me).

I have found that in the Thanking comes the Hope. Let me explain.... The Lord had told me to stop asking when it concerned my children (in a certain situation, NOT ALL) and just thank Him. I felt that He told me I had prayed every prayer I could pray; I had done everything I could do, NOW I was to thank Him. He revealed to me that I was in a state of heart sickness, then He led me to the above scripture. I recognized myself in the scripture...my hope had been deferred and now my heart was sick. So, I began to do what He told me and thank Him instead of asking again and again. I began to thank Him for those things that He had told me in the past that my children were. The things that had been spoken over them as young people, the things that they had dreams of doing as a child. I made lists of all the things I felt were God's will in their lives. Then I would Thank God that He was working those things out in their lives, even when I could see nothing. I thanked Him for drawing Himself unto them, even when they never mentioned a thing, I thanked Him for allowing them to find favor, even when I did not see it. It was a definite act of faith and trust!!

Now I cannot even explain to you what actually happened, except to say my hopelessness turned into an ETERNAL hope that's unexplainable. I found that after a few days of thanking Him my Hope had been restored.

The situation had not changed one bit, as far as I could see, but my Hope in what God could see and what He was doing had. WOW, WHO WOULDA THOUGHT??? All I did was change the direction of the prayer and HE DID THE REST!! My hope is no longer differed...it is right where it should be...My Hope Is in The Lord!! I'm still waiting for the "longing to be fulfilled" But in the mean time I HAVE HOPE!!!! ETERNAL HOPE!!!

Pause today and consider
Where you may have lost hope
Write down what you can thank God for

Dear Adonai,

Thank You for Your sweetness and peace! You are so faithful to watch over our hearts! Thank You so much for giving me encouragement from day to day. Thank You for Your Word which brings joy and fulness of life to my weary soul. Help me to continue to rely on You for my strength and hope, and not my circumstances. You are the Best!

In Jesus Name
AMEN

Suggested song: "My Hope Is In The Lord" by Sanctus Real/ Live Takeaway

DAY 12

TAKE YOUR HANDS OFF AND STEP BACK

W e've all heard the phrase "take your hands off and step back" or something similar when watching action dramas. It usually is at a very pivotal point in a movie, where the choice to step back or not determines life or death.

One of our favorite pass-times is going to see movies. My husband and I both enjoy them, that is a fun shared interest. He's taught me how to appreciate historical movies and I've taught him how to appreciate a girl flick!! BUT WE BOTH LOVE ACTION FILMS!!! The chase scenes, the thrills, the intrigue, the unexpected. It's all a blast!!! But as much as I like it in a film...I'm not so thrilled with it in my own life, OR AT LEAST I DON'T THINK I AM.

It does make you wonder sometimes doesn't it? Am I creating the drama I see in my life? and ask, why am I doing this?

We have seen a lot of drama in our lifetime, having been in ministry for over thirty-eight years has proved to be a means by which we have observed a lot of it. I have found that there are people who naturally bring on their own drama.

I have watched them create bigger issues for themselves than what is necessary, sometimes it would seem that they even thrive on drama.

> They can't seem to step back and take a breath, they just keep barking up the same tree, even when their prey is long gone. Then there are other times when that poor piece of "meat", they have targeted, just can't get away, and are trapped by this person's giant paw.

Hopefully you are not one of those, but if you are acting as one, then please step back.

God watches us and sometimes, if we are listening, we'll hear Him say "TAKE YOUR HANDS OFF AND STEP BACK"... At that point it's time to listen, or something worse could happen.

> *"Later Jesus found him at the temple and said to him,*
> *"See, you are well again.*
> *Stop sinning or something worse may happen to you."*
> **John 5:14** NIV

There are times when we choose to ignore the warning signs... But This Is Not One Of Those Times! If the Lord is telling you to take your hands off...THEN TAKE YOUR HANDS OFF!!!

It is very difficult to be in a situation that we have no control over, it causes us to feel helpless and victimized, when we, as the innocent bystander, want to take charge of the situation we find ourselves in (which is totally understandable!). The problem that occurs is when we think "I will force the person that has caused all this mess to "pay up" or else". Well, that just creates more friction in the situation. It also causes tempers to rise and the one thing that you need to keep in mind is that you are more than likely dealing with an unstable situation, if not an unstable person as well. Take that concern, anger and wrath to The Lord. He will sustain you! He will calm you! He will cause all things to work together for your good and the good of the person(s) involved. Don't risk the chance of making more of a mess!

> *"Consider it pure joy, my brothers and sisters,*
> *whenever you face trials of many kinds,*
> *because you know that the testing of your faith*
> *produces perseverance.*
> *Let perseverance finish its work so that you may be*
> *mature and complete,*
> *not lacking anything. If any of you lacks wisdom,*
> *you should ask God,*
> *Who gives generously to all without finding fault,*
> *and it will be given to you.*
> *But when you ask, you must believe and not doubt,*
> *because the one who doubts is like a wave of the sea,*
> *blown and tossed by the wind.*
> *That person should not expect to receive*
> *anything from the Lord.*
> *Such a person is double-minded*
> *and unstable in all they do."*
> **James 1:2**

Don't mess this "thing" up anymore then what it already is!! God's got this!! REALLY, HE DOES!! Your job is to step back and watch Him work, He really doesn't need your hands (OR MOUTH) in the middle of this. Ask Him for His wisdom, and EXPECT to receive it! Do not be double-minded yourself.

Is there any area where God is asking you to step back?
How can you take steps to be obedient?

Dear God,

Help me today to be obedient to what You are asking of me. Help me to know God, that You are trustworthy and help me Lord to take my hands off this situation today!! This situation does not need me, it needs You to intervene and make it all better!! I release this situation over to You today with the anticipation that You make all things new. Help me to be willing to stay out of Your way, as to not make things worse.

In Jesus Name
AMEN

Suggested song: "How He Loves" by David Crowder Band (K-Love)

Day 13

All a Matter of Perspective

Have you ever had a situation where someone tells you about an encounter that they had with another person? Their comment about that encounter goes like this "it seems really good to me, I felt really good about it!" but your perspective was totally different, your perspective didn't feel like it was such a good thing, it didn't feel like it was in that person's best interest.

That happened to me just recently and I came away from that moment asking God why do I feel this way? Why do I see it so differently than that person sees it? And I felt like maybe God was telling me that it was all in the perspective, my perspective was from a wounded perspective.

We must be aware that we can experience different types of wounds. There are wounds to our body that are superficial and Praise Be to God, they usually heal on their own very well, as long as we keep them clean. God made our bodies to heal naturally. Then there are wounds to our soul (mind, feelings, emotions). These wounds we may need to pray about, mainly so we stay in the right frame of mind, so it doesn't affect our attitude (or our will).

If we choose not to deal with those wounds properly, they can eventually escalate into a broken spirit, by that time you may be begging for death. NOW THAT IS A BROKEN SPIRIT!

Spirit wounds are deep wounds, that we might not even recognize are within us.

There are several scriptures in God's word that speaks about a broken spirit. From my observation of these scripture verses a broken spirit can be caused by others or caused by our utter exhaustion and exasperation.

This particular devotional is actually the last one that I wrote. I felt the Lord wanted me to write about this subject, but I needed time to wrap my brain around it and understand it even more. He would not allow me to take any shortcuts on this one, because it is so important for you to understand. So, I will be including many scriptures today. This could be a long one, so get ready!!

I wrote an email to Glory of Zion Ministries to "get their take" on the difference between a wounded soul and a wounded or broken spirit, this was the response I received…

"Biblically the heart is the place where you make decisions. It is interchangeable with the soul, which is the mind, emotions and will. A broken heart comes from disappointment, hope deferred, rejection and things like that.

Your spirit is the essence of who you are. It is the place of life. A broken spirit occurs when you have basically lost the desire to live, you do not see any point in trying to move forward."

> *"The spirit of a man will sustain him in sickness*
> *but **who can endure a broken spirit**?"*
> ***Prov. 18:14*** *NKJV*
> *(my emphasis added)*

This is exactly "where I was headed" with all of this. Thank you Linda for responding so quickly! (I literally received the email the day I was starting to write this day of the devotional)

Here is what we learn from scripture...

> *"A happy heart makes the face cheerful,*
> *but **heartache crushes the spirit**."*
> **Proverbs 15:13** NIV
> *(my emphasis added)*

> *"And Eli said to her, How long are you going to be the*
> *worse for drink? Put away the effects of your wine from*
> *you. And Hannah, answering him, said, No, my lord, I am*
> *a woman **whose spirit is broken with sorrow**:*
> *I have not taken wine or strong drink, but I have been*
> *opening my heart before the Lord."*
> **1 Samuel 1:14 -15** BBE
> *(my emphasis added)*

Hannah was so overcome with grief and sorrow, she was crying loudly before the Lord, from not being able to have a child. So much so, that she looked drunk to Eli.

In Jobs **anguish** he cried out to God...

> *"**My spirit is broken**, my days are cut short,*
> *the grave awaits me.*
> *Surely mockers surround me;*
> *my eyes must dwell on their hostility."*
> **Job 17:1**
> *(my emphasis added)*

And later as Job was defending himself, he says...

> *"if I have devoured its yield without payment or*
> **broken the spirit of its tenants"**
> **Job 31:39** NIV
> *(my emphasis added)*

... in other words, he could cause a broken spirit.

> *"Moses spoke thus to the people of Israel,*
> *but they did not listen to Moses,*
> **because of their broken spirit and harsh slavery."**
> **Exodus 6:9** ESVUK
> *(my emphasis added)*

The Israelites were so overworked that they just wanted to give up, they did not want Moses to "get their hopes up", so they didn't even listen to him.

> *"A cheerful heart is good medicine,*
> *but a **crushed spirit dries up the bones.**"*
> **Proverbs 17:22** NIV
> *(my emphasis added)*

> *"Near is Jehovah to the* **broken of heart**
> **and the bruised of spirit** *He saveth."*
> **Psalm 34:18** YLT
> *(my emphasis added)*

I like that translation because it shows that we can have a bruised spirit, and as you know to be bruised means that some sort of impact has caused a temporary scar. But Jehovah is near to us when we experience hurt and He saves us from the bruises as well!

CAUSES

An intense heartache can cause a broken spirit, intense sorrow can cause a broken spirit, intense anguish and questioning (questioning everything that you have formerly believed) can cause a broken spirit. As well as being physically, emotionally or verbally abused to such an extent that it causes a broken spirit.

"WHO CAN BEAR IT?"

AFFECT

It dries up our bones. The sorrow and anguish are so intense it brings us to a place of feeling death is near.

RESPONSE

Is Gods...

> *"**The Lord is close** to the brokenhearted*
> *and saves those who are crushed in spirit."*
> ***Psalms 34:18*** *NIV*
> *(my emphasis added)*

Then in the next two verses we are reminded to "Look up" ... the Lord does not want us to focus on our issues, but to look up to Him! He does not want us so overwhelmed that our spirits break. He wants us to be reminded of who He is and what He has done throughout time (before time began). As well as what He will do and what He will continue to do!!

> *"Lift up your eyes and look to the heavens:*
> *Who created all these?*
> *He who brings out the starry host one by one*
> *and calls forth each of them by name.*
> *Because of His great power and mighty strength,*
> *not one of them is missing."*
> ***Isaiah 40:26*** *NIV*
> *(my emphasis added)*

> *"Lift up your eyes and look around;*
> *all your children gather and come to you.*
> *As surely as I live,"* **declares the Lord,**
> *"you will wear them all as ornaments;*
> *you will put them on, like a bride."*
> **Isaiah 49:8** *NIV*
> *(my emphasis added)*

> *"The Lord said to Abram after Lot had parted from him,*
> *"Look around from where you are,*
> *to the north and south, to the east and west.*
> *All the land that you see I will give to you*
> *and your offspring forever.*
> *I will make your offspring like the dust of the earth, so*
> *that if anyone could count the dust,*
> *then your offspring could be counted.*
> *Go, walk through the length and breadth of the land, for I*
> *am giving it to you."*
> **Genesis 13:15**

This is our encouragement, after Abraham saw that Lot chose the best of the land, the Lord turned around and gave him everything else plus a promise that would last forever! He also instructed Abraham to "walk through...the land". This is a very important key to victory. What is a "walk-through"? It is a rehearsal! WOOHOO!!! God wants us to practice our future victories even before it's "official"! That's what God wants to do for us. He wants to give us everything the locust has eaten, He wants to restore our spirit to have life and to have life abundantly, He wants us to thank Him and rejoice in advance. He wants to see us joyful and full of His glory FOREVER!!

> *"Come close to God and God will come close to you."*
> **James 4:8a** *NLT*

"The Lord helps the fallen and
lifts those bent beneath their loads."
Psalms 145:14 NLT

Today I suggest you take the sorrow and pain you feel,
Allow The Lord to lift the load
That you have been bent under
Crawl up into your Heavenly Fathers lap
Allow Him to comfort you and stroke your hair
Allow Him to kiss your head and tell you "it will be alright!"
Allow Him to draw close

Dear El Roi,

Thank You for watching over us, thank You that Your care about our spirits even more than we do! Thank You that You are here to draw near to us and comfort us in this time of uncertainty! Thank You that You are able to lift this load I've been bent under! Help me to rejoice in advance and trust You for what You have promised.

In Jesus Name

Suggested song: "Rescue" by NewSong

DAY 14

STICK WITH IT

What compels you to "stick with it"? HOPEFULLY it is the greatness and goodness of our God. But when you're in the middle of circumstances that are difficult, that you didn't ask for, that you actually prayed against, do you feel like you don't want to hold on any longer? Are you too exhausted, because of your circumstance?

I recall at one point on this journey saying to the Lord, "I feel as if I have been backed up into a corner, and have no strength to fight. I'm gonna lift up the Shield of Faith and just stay here for a bit, if You don't mind". I am sure He smiled at me that day, and said "If that's where you want to be today, that's fine, you get some rest, just don't plan on staying there!" So, if you need a day to rest to hide behind your shield of faith, then go ahead, but after you've rested, come out with your full armor on and guns blazing. Because that is not the place for a warrior, in a corner. Come out knowing that…

The greatness and goodness of our God should compel us!

Many years ago, we were visiting our family, while my brother-in-law, David, who was the pastor of a church in Oregon, was suffering from cancer.

By this point in his cancer journey, his body was racked by the cancer, it was obvious his strength was gone, and he was wasting away before our eyes. But in the middle of all of that, as he was speaking to his congregation, expressing how "Our God is worthy of our praise, how can we not stand to give Him our wholehearted praise?", he was determined to stand and give his God praise, even when his body tried to restrain him.

> *"Sing to the Lord, all the earth;*
> *proclaim His salvation Day after day.*
> *Declare His glory among the nations,*
> *His marvelous deeds among all peoples.*
> *For great is the Lord and most worthy of praise;*
> *He is to be feared above all gods.*
> *For all the gods of the nations are idols,*
> *but the Lord made the heavens.*
> *Splendor and majesty are before Him;*
> *strength and joy are in His dwelling place.*
> *Ascribe to the Lord, all you families of nations,*
> *ascribe to the Lord glory and strength.*
> *Ascribe to the Lord the glory due His name;*
> *bring an offering and come before Him.*
> *Worship the Lord in the splendor of His holiness.*
> *Tremble before Him, all the earth!*
> *The world is firmly established; it cannot be moved.*
> *Let the heavens rejoice, let the earth be glad;*
> *let them say among the nations,*
> *"The Lord reigns!" Let the sea resound, and all that is in it;*
> *let the fields be jubilant, and everything in them!*
> *Let the trees of the forest sing,*
> *let them sing for joy before the Lord,*
> *for He comes to judge the earth.*
> *Give thanks to the Lord, for He is good;*
> *His love endures forever."*
> **1 Chronicles 16:23**
> (my emphasis added)

What about Him compels you to continue on? Why do you stick with it? Is it all worth it? Ask yourself the hard questions today, BUT make sure that you come to the conclusion of Our God is Great! Our God is good! Our God is mighty! Our God can do this! Our God can handle this situation! Our God is a great, awesome, mighty, compassionate, merciful, loving God. That's why we go on and pull up our bootstraps and face another day, because He is worth it! Because He is glorious, because He is wonderful, because He is mighty, because He is good, because He is kind, BECAUSE HE LOVES US MORE THAN OUR MINDS CAN CONCIEVE!!!! AND CARES ABOUT THE "MESSES" IN OUR LIVES MORE THAN WE OURSELVES!

That moment, witnessing the determination of my brother-in-law, is a time that has always given me pause. Today it's time to push the pause button and consider HIM.... His greatness is why we're even here. His love and His mercy, His compassion for us is what gives us strength to face another day.

*Spend time today thinking on
The greatness and goodness of God*

Lord,

We stand today, we just want to spend time thanking You today! Thank You, that You give us times to rest and gather our thoughts and strength. Help me to not stay in that place, but to come out on the other side filled with Your strength and power. Thank You for who you are! You are worthy of every bit of praise we can give You! You are our Great and Mighty God, You are worthy of all praise, honor and thanksgiving. You are Holy, You are Awesome, You are Faithful, You are trustworthy. You are more than our minds can conceive! Thank You Lord for who You are. I praise You God our Creator, our Redeemer, our Sustainer, our Mighty Fortress, the God in Whom we put all of our trust.

In Jesus Name
AMEN

Suggested song: "When I think About The Lord" by Christ for the Nations

DAY 15

. . .

SAY WHAT?

What a difficult discussion we had with our son. I came away thinking "WHERE IN THE WORLD DID YOU GROW UP?" Oh, my goodness.... what an utter disappointment to hear "well, we can't really be sure of our salvation" WHAT? AGAIN WHAT????? Our response was "ummm, WE ARE!!!" WOW, TRULY UNBELIEVABLE!!!

SO, here's our story...my husband was raised in an Assemblies of God church all his life. It was before there were pastors hired for every different ministry in a church. His parents were very involved "pillars of the church", his dad basically held every position but senior pastor, with his wife supporting him all the way! He (my husband) was always well grounded in Christ and went on into "Ministry" (as well as his older siblings). I on the other hand, was raised Lutheran and really didn't come to Christ until I was fourteen, but was very committed and knew from a young age (sixteen) that I was going to be a "Pastors wife". I was also very involved with my Church and very committed to Christ (other than one year of pure rebellion at age seventeen).

We met, were married and promptly moved to another city for my husband to become a youth pastor. We raised our children

61

to believe in and trust in THE ONLY TRUE GOD, JESUS!!! So, to hear anything contrary to what we taught them is very hard to take!!! Where do they get this stuff??? I know it's not from God's word! Which leads me to my theme for today.

Raise your children to be VERY aware of who they're befriending!!! (we thought we did). Our children would tell you that we watched over them like hawks. We have watched both our children choose friends and relationships, even those in the church that we "checked out" for ourselves, but they ended up to be wrong influences, they were in no way living for Christ, and that's what our children seemed to be drawn to. It is so difficult to explain to kids how their friends will influence them one way or another. BUT THEY DO!! Sometimes they don't even act like they know God. Did they ever? I thought they did, but now I'm questioning everything!!

Now, I know that some of you have even worse stories than ours, and for that I'm truly sorry!!! I have had friends tell me that their kids won't even mention Christ and don't want to "hear it". How sad! We can at least talk to our kids about Christ, they don't totally shut us down. BUT my point is "how did they get to this point?" When did the opinions of their non-Christian friends become more important than God's Word? How did they even get to the point of thinking "yea, maybe the Word of God isn't all true, or worth living for!" My heart is SO SAD!!

Some may think, what a waste of time! You dedicated your lives to God and poured into your children for so many years, only for them to choose the world. I know that it may look grim to outsiders, BUT WE HAVE A SPECIAL WEAPON!! We know this weapon well! He's not a secret, because He has made Himself, and His ways, very clear and easy to understand. All His info is in His Word, The Holy Bible.

I am not overwhelmed; I am not giving up because...

I KNOW THAT MY GOD REDEEMS WHAT THE LOCUST HAS EATEN!!! HE RESTORES AND GIVES US BLESSINGS BEYOND

OUR IMAGINATIONS!!! So, I will not fear! I will not be dismayed!! For my God is the redeemer of all. PRAISE BE TO GOD WHO REDEEMS MY CHILDREN'S LIVES FROM THE PIT!!!!

> *"I will repay you for the years the locusts have eaten"*
> **Joel 2:25** *NIV*

If you are not aware, the "locust" here represents our enemy, which is Satan himself. he has nothing on the God of the universe. Trust me, he'll be sorry for messing with me!!

Where could you lean on The Lord more?

Dear Lord,

Thank You that You are the "weapon of choice". You are Christ, Christ is the Word and the Word is our weapon. Thank You for continually pointing me in the right direction and I ask that You will give me eyes to see, and ears to hear ALWAYS! Thank You that I can trust You with my children and that I can trust You to keep me steady, when everything around me can feel shaky. Help me not to be overwhelmed with the circumstances around me, but to lean on You fully.

In Jesus Name
AMEN

Suggested song: "The Best Is Yet To Come" by Donald Lawrence/ Go Get Your Life Back album

***I just want to take this opportunity to encourage any of you who may be reading this book, because of your overwhelming situation, but have never given your whole heart to God. It is not to late! And this is the time!

Now is the day to give it all to Christ!

Please if you have never prayed a prayer of repentance and total surrender, I have included a prayer at the back of this book for you to do just that.

DAY 16

HIS ROD AND STAFF

I once had an encounter with a friend who explained a situation concerning her adult daughter. She proceeded to tell me how she was dealing with the situation and apparently how she was going to continue to deal with the situation. She asked what I thought she should do. "Well, because you asked..." I began explaining why I thought that maybe she should take a different approach and that because her daughter was an adult, just maybe she should let God handle it. Needless to say, that particular conversation ended pretty quick and was never spoken of again. I really don't know how it turned out.

What is obvious to me though, because I've made the same mistake myself, is that we can so easily get in God's way when we want to take matters into our own hands. We can make a bigger mess than what is already existing. We may even risk the chance of an irreparable situations occurring.

I love how God uses everything in our lives to draw us unto Himself. If we are in tune to Holy Spirit, He will open our eyes to the things, or circumstances, around us and point us to Himself.

In my life He has used children, furniture, appliances, vehicles, traffic and animals, to name a few. He wants us to be fully aware of His presence in our lives every minute of the day.

If you just think about the love that a dog has for his master, it makes you want to be like that with our Heavenly Father. The love and devotion dogs show to us is astounding!! They get so excited when we return home, they follow us everywhere in the house, they lay down when we rest and love us unconditionally. However, on the other hand they can "look" like us in so many ways. They may be stubborn and not follow our direction, they may only want to walk around the block a certain way, they may want to run, when we want to walk. They are a perfect example of what we can look like.

I wanted to do a little research for this particular devotional, so I looked up on YouTube about shepherds and sheep. I found two examples I want to share with you today, please go to YouTube and look up...

*** "The good shepherd and his sheep" (with this one you need to turn on the "captions" before pushing play (three little dots up in right corner-in the list), it's in another language.

*** "Do sheep only obey their master's voice"

ISN'T THAT AMAZING??? I love to see examples of God's word illustrated in our daily lives!!

When we don't listen to our Heavenly Father, we not only get left out of what He has for us, but it is sinning. And sometimes He speaks through others to hint to us what He prefer we do. Don't get me wrong, I am not saying that I was right, in that situation I explained, or that I am always right, and that everyone needs to do what I say. Oh, dear God, no!!! What I am saying is that we need to keep our ears open to what the Spirit is saying (and He may use someone else's mouth), and you will know that voice when you hear it. "My sheep listen to my voice".

> *"Even though I walk through the darkest valley,*
> *I will fear no evil, for You are with me;*
> *Your rod and Your staff, they comfort me."*
> **Psalms 23:4** NIV
> *(my emphasis added)*

In these moments we should be reminded how our Shepherd at times uses His rod, which is to ward off the enemy, and then there are times He uses His staff, to pull us out of danger or on to the path He would prefer us to be on. May we ever be aware, and our ears attune to our Shepherd, then all you have to do is ask God what's next?

I encourage you today to take a moment
And listen for The Shepherds voice
What do you hear?

Dear loving Shepherd,

Thank You for Your rod and staff that comforts and leads me! Thank You that You don't leave me to my own devices, but that You will forever encourage me to take the path that You know is good and safe. Please help me to hear Your voice when You speak and especially help me to recognize it when You speak through someone else. Give me a heart that receives correction and that welcomes change. Help me to always be willing to adjust my responses accordingly when they don't line up to Yours.

In Jesus Name
AMEN

Suggested Song: "Symphony" by Dillon Chase, Switch

DAY 17

WEARY AND WOUNDED

D o you find yourself wounded, and weary? Do you believe this could be a result of something you're doing? Or do you believe this is a result of someone else's doing?

It's not usually hard to determine where our hurts and wounds come from. BUT WHY CAN'T WE JUST SWEEP THEM AWAY? And the weariness, where does that come from?

I have been praying for one of my friends a young man that I've known since he was a teen. As I was praying for him the Lord showed me that he was refusing HIS healing. He was so angry with God and so determined not to forgive that God could not move forward to heal his heart. What an awful place to be! Isn't it interesting how we can forever blame everyone and the devil for our circumstances! Yet, maybe we need to examine the stubbornness of our own heart!

> *"Search me, God, and know my heart;*
> *test me and know my anxious thoughts.*
> *See if there is any offensive way in me,*
> *and lead me in the way everlasting"*
> **Psalm 139:23** NIV

Before I left home and went to my one year of college. I had been in a very fallen state, I had stopped going to church, I ignored my Christian friends, I was all consumed with a guy in my life that I was enamored with. However, God did not let me stay there, He brought me back to a place of seeing! He actually gave me a dream of what my life would look like if I stayed in that relationship. So, I told the Lord "I'm not going to be able to break-up, You are going to have to do this". You see, I THOUGHT I was in love!

God did it! He caused the guy to break up with me… What was interesting about it was, as he's breaking off our "engagement", he said these words "I don't know why I am doing this!" Well, I DID!! And to make a long story longer… I went off to bible college and that's where God transformed my life. I always say I paid $2,000 to come back to Christ (yes, that was a long time ago!) In one night, I was changed and it was all due to Holy Spirit and Psalms 139. It is such a calming assurance of where God has been throughout your life. Please read it all! And by the end in verse 23, you are ready to ask for change. We need to allow God to search our hearts, sometimes He will show us why we chose what we chose, and how those choices caused wounds, sorrow and anxiousness. After I read Ps. 139, God also showed me where He was the entire time I had walked away from serving Him. He was right near me, tapping my shoulder, trying to get my attention. I was oblivious, but He was near, and He never gave up! I love how David goes into a little rant about his enemies right in the middle of exaltation to the Lord, but then quickly refocuses and says "search me".

When we allow the anxious thoughts to take over, we are allowing the enemy to have a foothold into our lives. We can so easily spin out of control when we are anxious (now I know there are those out there that understand what I am talking about, I can't be the only one!)

*"Do not be anxious about anything,
but in every situation, by prayer and petition,
with thanksgiving, present your request to God.
And the peace of God,
which transcends all understanding,
will guard your hearts and your minds in Christ Jesus."*
Philippians 4:6-7 NIV

*Allow The Lord to "search" your heart
Allow Him to shine a spotlight
Into every room and crevice
Repent of anything He shows you
Then finish with our prayer
Go and be led in "the way everlasting"*

Oh Lord,

May I never get in Your way, may I submit every thought and word to You. Help me, oh God, not to sabotage my own progress with unforgiveness and anger. Break off the rebellious, prideful spirit that I have been permitting in my life and replace them with humbleness and obedience. Thank You Jesus for your forgiveness and for giving me a brand-new start.

In Jesus Name
AMEN

Suggested song: "Psalms 40" by NewSong

DAY 18

ALL HOPE IS LOST

Have you ever been afraid to hope?

It's a difficult place to be, when you don't even want to hope anymore because you've been let down so many times. There are times when we have to fight to hope.

Fighting is a difficult thing, it's not easy! If you look at the way our military treats fighting, they don't just throw an untrained person in the middle of a battle. First, they go through training, they go through all kinds of drills and battle scenarios, the trainers even go as far as to deny them food and water so they're prepared for the battle.

It's not only the battle that's hard but the training is hard as well. I am absolutely sure that soldiers get sick of training!!

When I feel I am going through a training process, that's how I feel, I get very sick of the training, and I just want it to be over. But if we are honest, we tend to think EVERYTHING is a battle, when its actually just a training drill, because it's so hard and so realistic, it feels like the real thing.

The moment we realize "oh that was just a drill" is when we are actually in the middle of the real battle.

At that point, we are very thankful for the training that the Lord was gracious enough to allow us to go through, and not only that, but to go through it with us. To imagine that I am just in training for the battle could be daunting, maybe that's why we don't seem to recognize it until later. The battles are always more intense than the training, that is why the training is so important!

My hopes have been dashed so often and so thoroughly that it's hard for me to imagine hoping anymore. But I must trust in God's word, I must go forward, I must believe what His word says is true, even in the midst of despair and sorrow. I imagine that these are the same sort of thoughts that a solider must face when in the midst of battle, they must rely on what they have been trained to do, not the feelings they are feeling in the midst of darkness. I must put my trust in the one who sees and keeps me going, that is my God! TODAY THIS IS MY BATTLE, TO HOPE WHEN ALL HOPE SEEMS LOST!! He has trained me for this!

> *"But we have this treasure in jars of clay*
> *to show that this all-surpassing power*
> *is from God and not from us.*
> *We are hard pressed on every side, but not crushed;*
> *perplexed, but not in despair;*
> *persecuted, but not abandoned;*
> *struck down, but not destroyed."*
> ***2 Corinthians 4:7***

All of chapter 4 is worth the read (as is all the Bible).

> *"I lift up my eyes to the mountains—*
> *where does my help come from?*
> *My help comes from the Lord,*
> *the Maker of heaven and earth.*
> *He will not let your foot slip—*
> *He who watches over you will not slumber;*
> *indeed, He who watches over Israel*
> *will neither slumber nor sleep.*

The Lord watches over you—
the Lord is your shade at your right hand;
the sun will not harm you by day, nor the moon by night.
The Lord will keep you from all harm—
He will watch over your life;
the Lord will watch over your coming and going
both now and forevermore."
Psalm 121:1
(my emphasis added)

Look back on where you have come form
And what God has taught you
Write them down to remind yourself of His goodness

Dear Heavenly Father,

I praise You for who You are and how you always go before me and how I can be secure in the training that You have given me. I ask that You will continue to give me the strength I need to continue on through any battle I face. Please help me to recall all the lessons of the training You have allowed me to undergo, and respond accordingly. I ask that You will help me to keep my eyes on You, where my help comes from!

In Jesus Name
AMEN

Suggested Song: "I Will Lift Mine Eyes" by Andrae Crouch (from "First Love" Album)

HIS WORD DOES NOT RETURN VOID!!!!!

W e raised our children *"in the training and instruction of the Lord" Eph. 6:4 NIV*, yet we find ourselves wondering "what happened?". They don't seem to have the same convictions we have; they don't seem to have time for the Lord we raised them to serve, and it would seem as if they really don't care. BUT I know that this is not really the case! That is just how the enemy wants us to see it. That is not the true picture!

Have you ever seen an episode of "Fake or Fortune"? This is a program produced by the BBC that searches out if a painting is fake or if it is worth something less or more than expected. In the intro of this program you hear "every picture tells its own story, and it's up to us to try and uncover it". Well, I would venture to say that the same is true for each person that lives on this planet earth. The difference is that it's not up to us to uncover "it" in the lives of others, it's up to Holy Spirit to uncover it to each individual person. You see for us to "uncover" the secrets of another would put too much responsibility on us as the outsiders. To allow Holy Spirit to do His work leaves the outcome to Him and that person.

> *"For My thoughts are not your thoughts,*
> *neither are your ways My ways," declares the Lord.*
> *"As the heavens are higher than the earth,*
> *so are My ways higher than your ways*
> *and My thoughts than your thoughts.*
> *As the rain and the snow come down from heaven,*
> *and do not return to it without watering the earth*
> *and making it bud and flourish,*
> *so that it yields seed for the sower and bread for the eater,*
> *so is My word that goes out from My mouth:*
> *It will not return to Me empty, but will accomplish what I*
> *desire and achieve the purpose for which I sent it.*
> *You will go out in joy and be led forth in peace;*
> *the mountains and hills will burst into song before you,*
> *and all the trees of the field will clap their hands.*
> *Instead of the thorn bush will grow the cypress,*
> *and instead of briers the myrtle will grow.*
> *This will be for the Lord 's renown, for an everlasting sign,*
> *that will endure forever."*
> **Isaiah 55: 8-13** NIV
> *(my emphasis added)*

Cypress tree is an evergreen, it grows fast, it likes swampy water soil, it enjoys the sun, it is beautiful and even though it is a fast grower it has a very hard wood, which is not typical of fast growers. Not only is it a hard wood, But IT'S A VERY DESIRED HARD WOOD. It also sheds its needles in the winter but in the spring grows beautiful foliage, and in the fall, that same foliage has a very beautiful rust color. IT ADAPTS TO THE SEASONS!

Myrtle is a beautiful and fragrant evergreen tree, growing wild throughout the southern parts of Europe, the north of Africa, and the temperate parts of Asia; principally on the seacoast. The leaves are of a rich and polished evergreen.

It is so interesting to me that instead of thorns and briers there will be strong everlasting, fruit bearing, fragrant trees. Go God!!

How encouraging to know that "Those Words" that we raised our children on WILL NOT RETURN VOID TO THE LORD!!!! HALLELUJAH!!!

My responsibility to these children of mine (now that they are adults) is to continue to lift them up in prayer and allow them enough "space" to make decisions for Christ on their own. If they would come to me and ask for help, I would certainly be there giving any answers I could within a split second, but until then Holy Spirit can handle this job. It will never be overwhelming to Him!! Instead of the thorn bush, that we "seem" to see and feel, will be a beautiful cypress that adapts to every season. And instead of the briars (or their actions or mistakes that seem to attach themselves to us or their own lives) there will be a wonderful everlasting fragrance that penetrates the atmosphere!

"This will be for the Lord's renown"!!!!

Spend time today thanking God for His plans
That are continually going forth in making your loved one(s)
Into the "Cypress and Myrtle"

Oh Lord,

You are worthy of all praise and honor. You are the King of kings and Lord of lords. You are the Everlasting Living Word that does not return void! Thank You for reminding us, with Your Word, that You will make all those we concern ourselves with new, brand new, into what You always intended them to be!! And that You will bless all of us with them!

You are our Awesome Adonai!!!!

AMEN

Suggested song: "Seasons" by Donald Lawrence/Go Get Your Life Back album

DAY 20

YOUR GRACE IS ENOUGH

Did you wake up this morning to a darker world than yesterday?

Now, everyone in our world could answer an emphatic YES! But there are those of us who actually do wake up to deeper and darker situations than we did the day before. Just when it seems it can't get any worse, "surely God does not think that I can handle one more thing! ", it happens, it gets worse. Our day just got darker; our future seems to be unreachable. It would seem that we will forever be stuck on this proverbial hamster wheel and never get anywhere. Why God? Why would you allow this?

There's not always an answer right away for that one. As a matter of fact, you may need to wait quite a while before you get an answer, or it may never be answered. But there will be a day when you look back and ponder it, and what you'll see is God's Grace. Thru it all His Grace is at work. He gives us strength to face another day and the grace we need to make decisions we didn't even ask to make, all while we feel stumped and in the dark. There are days I wake up singing "Your Grace Is Enough". That is what literally gets me through that day. The Lord himself told us…

"My grace is sufficient for you".
2 Corithiansn12:9 *NIV*

Well if the Lords said it, I believe it, and it can happen!!

Don't allow the dark circumstances of your day to cloud your vision. Allow God to give you His grace to see a bright future and the clear path that leads there.

Recently I spent an entire day overcome with grief, that grief was my companion for the day. I say it this way because, not realizing what I was allowing, I just kept "grief" close by my side that day. I couldn't stop crying, I was overwhelmed, I was questioning every move and every decision. Then I texted my prayer partners (I happen to have a number of friends, that I can call on to intercede for me...AND I DID!). I knew this was not a "place" that God wanted me in and I needed to leave AND NOW! With my prayer support I made it through that day!! Thank God for friends who genuinely care!!!! I came away from that day thanking God for all the people in our life that continually pray for us. I knew beyond a shadow of a doubt that their prayers helped me that day and all the days that led up to that one!

Just yesterday we went to see a movie, it was about WWII, there were several scenes where a young man, who fell in love with a young woman, but was more concerned about himself and his cause then her. He kept saying this phrase over and over to her "my little comrade ". Every time he said it, it made me cringe! He targeted her, became her companion and then put her in danger.

> *"Be alert and of sober mind. Your enemy the devil*
> *prowls around*
> *like a roaring lion looking for someone to devour."*
> ***1 Peter 5:8*** *NIV*

The enemy most times comes in as a companion. He wants you to think he's on your side, but it's just a ploy to use you and eventually take you down. The enemy can come in as a thought or as a real person. You can recognize those people by how you feel as you walk away. If you ever have a "sinking" feeling as you walk away, keep walking!

Paul gives us a glimpse of this...

> *"For such people are false apostles, deceitful workers, masquerading as apostles of Christ. And no wonder, for Satan himself masquerades as an angel of light."*
> **II Corinthians 11: 13 &14** NIV

Look back on those moments in your life
That God has given you His grace to go through
Ask God to remind you of where His has always been
During those dark times of your life

Dear Heavenly Father,

Thank You so much for giving us "fair warning" in Your Word! We are so thankful for the clarity that You give us as we read and obey Your word. Thank You for the friends You put in our lives to help us get through those very rough days, that each of us has. Most of all thank You for Holy Spirit, Who brings us Your Shalom and strength, so we can still be filled with Your Joy during these dark days!! Bless Your Holy Name!!

In Jesus Name
AMEN

Suggested song: "Your Grace Is Enough" by Matt Maher

DAY 21

ALL HAVE SINNED

I realize this book is written because of what the Lord told us to do with our son. But this also deals with our daughter, we have two children that as I can see have not totally walked away from the Lord, but they are not choosing to live their lives out for the Lord either. As we celebrated the Christmas season this year, I became very aware of the void of my children's presence. I love having my family around me during the Christmas season and any season for that matter. I enjoy my family tremendously. I enjoy sharing moments of life with them, laughing with them joking with them playing games and having fun with them, I enjoy them! But I very much missed them this year. I love having them sitting next to me during church services. I was especially reminded of their "distance" when I was sitting by myself during the holidays. My husband is on staff at the church; therefore, he is not always sitting next to me during services. But when the kids were young, they were always there next to me I really miss that!

Now before you start judging us, not knowing our family life. Please do not let your mind be led astray to thoughts from the enemy that would accuse us of having any kind of dysfunctional family life.

WE DID NOT! I know we all have moments in our families that seem dysfunctional, and I would suppose that is normal. But when we hear of families where their children are not serving the Lord, we are tempted to assume that there was some kind of dysfunction during these children's childhoods, or they would be serving the Lord. But this is not necessarily true!

A long time ago the Lord told me "Do not take on the responsibility of your adult children's decisions". Our children's lives and lifestyles do not reflect how they were raised, and that is not easy to accept. But these are the choices of their adulthood and we must live with these choices until God changes them. But let us not be found guilty of accusing others whether it be our own family members, or acquaintances in church, that there's something wrong in their family otherwise their children would be living for the Lord.

> *"Do not judge, or you too will be judged.*
> *For in the same way you judge others,*
> *you will be judged, and with the measure you use,*
> *it will be measured to you."*
> **Matthew 7:1**

OUCH!!! That was my first response when the Lord spoke that to me! Throughout this journey, and especially at the beginning, I was reminded of this verse continually! Not because the Lord wants us to feel condemned, but because He wants us to be able to improve with His correction.

When we choose the path of judging, ridicule, wrath, bitterness, anger or unforgiveness, we choose strife. We are causing ourselves to be "unsettled", we are choosing chaos instead of peace. You are actually choosing wickedness. Oh my, that is hard to receive, but it is soooooo true!! God's desire for us is to remain in Peace (or Shalom).

I have a Bible version called the One New Man Bible (distributed by Sid Roth ministries). I love my Bible, because it brings more knowledge of Jewish tradition (bible times and now) and definitions. The definition for the word Shalom is this...

"an absence of: disorder, injustice, bribery, corruption, conflict, lack, hatred, abuse, violence, pain, suffering, and all other negative forces. A rabbi wrote that Shalom means "No good thing is withheld.""

I LOVE that last quote! If we want to find peace, we must not withhold any good thing! When we find ourselves dealing with unreasonable people in our lives, we can tend to feel that they do not deserve anything "good" from us. But that does not line up with Gods ways. His ways do not withhold any good thing, no matter who they are. I do not remember ever being taught that in church!! DO YOU? Lessons like this were always based on Old Testament, where God had placed all the "If you will's" in His precepts and statutes. But when Jesus came, we see He freely gave to good and "bad" people alike.

> *"There is no peace," says the Lord, "for the wicked."*
> **Isaiah 48:22** *NIV*

So, I want to encourage you today to choose peace. Do not be counted among the wicked! But among those whose lives are grounded in Gods precepts.

> *"For all have sinned and fall short of the glory of God"*
> **Romans 3:23** *NIV*

I will admit it to you right now, I judged others when I should not have, others that found themselves in the same place I now find myself in. That hurts my heart! Let me assure you, if you judge, it WILL come back to you! Just as God's Word states in Matthew 7! BUT GOD, He walks us through our mistakes and gives us His grace to get us on the other side of them. That's where I am at now, on the other side of my sin. Forgiven and recovering! That makes my feet want to dance!!

Ask God where you may have been judgmental in the past
Ask Him to break off all the "chains"
That have held you back because of it
Ask Him to help you as you go forward
FREEDOM

Dear Abba,

Thank You for your continued relentlessness to not leave us behind because of our sin, but to inform us and transform us by the renewing of our minds. Help me to recognize any sins that Your mercy shows me. Help me to immediately ask for Your forgiveness and then please transform my thinking, so that I don't have any repeat performances and so I might live in Your peace. Forgive me today for any sins I may have committed in the process of my life. Please help me to forgive myself as well. Thank You for the blood of Jesus that makes me whiter than snow!! I SOOOOOO LOVE YOU LORD!!!!

In Jesus Name
AMEN

Suggested song: "Sometimes My Feet Want To Dance" by Gaither Vocal Band (Southern Classics album)

DAY 22

ON THE ROCK

One of my favorite memories of family time, is when we used to take a family trip every year to Wisconsin Dells with our children. We always had such an anticipation of the fun we would have for that week, and we were ALL excited. We were so blessed to have friends that would allow us to stay at their "Cabin" (the structure changed through the years, but we still called it a cabin). We stayed there so often that we asked them why our name wasn't carved in a wood plaque like all the rest of their family.

That was always an exciting trip, but one year we had gotten a new Andrae Crouch CD, and played it all the way there. There was a song on that album that to this day I use as a word picture for what God does for us. I drove our kids crazy with it, because I would gesture with my hands while I was singing and they would say "mom, stop", maybe because I would do it in their faces.

So, every time I am feeling like I am "going down", like I just can't do this anymore, when the circumstances of life have brought me to what feels, at that moment, like the point of death. The Lord reminds me of those moments and that particular line of the song, and I begin to feel His transforming power.

"The Lord is my light and my salvation—
whom shall I fear?
The Lord is the stronghold of my life—
of whom shall I be afraid?
When the wicked advance against me to devour me,
it is my enemies and my foes who will stumble and fall.
Though an army besiege me, my heart will not fear;
though war break out against me,
even then I will be confident.
One thing I ask from the Lord, this only do I seek:
that I may dwell in the house of the Lord
all the days of my life,
to gaze on the beauty of the Lord
and to seek Him in his temple.
For in the Day of trouble He will keep me safe in
His dwelling;
He will hide me in the shelter of His sacred tent
and set me high upon a rock.
Then my head will be exalted above the enemies
who surround me;
at His sacred tent I will sacrifice with shouts of joy;
I will sing and make music to the Lord."
Psalms 27:1
(my emphasis added)

The Pastor of our church recently spoke on Psalm 23. Now most of us have recited this scripture all of our lives, it's just one of those that, if you were in Sunday School as a child everyone had to memorize. In referring to the portion of scripture that says "Yeah, though I walk through the valley of the shadow of death, I will fear no evil", our pastor brought out a concept I had never thought about (Thank you Pastor John). The concept is this... The "shadow of death" is not speaking of literal death, it's referring to a "shadow", it's referring to "something that has the appearance of" death. WOW!!!!

David, in Psalms 23 was trying to make us recognize that we will have days where we will "feel" like we are going to die, BUT ITS JUST A SHADOW OF DEATH, and we do not need to fear. And again, in Psalms 27 he reminds us of our Great Protector.

In the song I like, the line that always made me do the hand gestures was "He puts me on a rock, out of the reach of them all", (this is where I would reach out my entire arm (into my children's faces), as if I couldn't reach something...but inferring that the enemy couldn't reach me! Then it goes on... "when my enemy tries to hurt me, I don't have to worry, I'm in his care not just here, but everywhere." Oh, I could go on and on with that song!!! I Love It!! I hope you'll listen to it later; I hope you enjoy it as much as I do!

The point is He; our Heavenly Father will protect us. Whether it be from an accident, or from a "feeling" of death or from the enemy himself, He Is There for us!!!

Take a moment today to see yourself on "The Rock"
Where the enemy can't reach you
Now Rejoice!!

Dear Abba,

Thank You for Your protection. Thank You for watching over me as I walk through this hard place. Help me to always be aware of Your presence and to know that You will keep me in Christ (the rock), out of the reach of my enemy! May Your Shalom rest upon me today and lead me out of all darkness into Your marvelous light.

In Jesus Name
AMEN

Suggested song: "The Lord is My Light" by Andrae Crouch

WHO'S DOING THE EDITTING

Does it seem to you that your prodigal's life right now is just "Baby Steps"? Don't you just want to kick them in the rear and say "GET ON WITH IT!!"?

We are avid movie goers...one of our "distractions"! When you see well made movies, you are hard pressed to know where they edited anything in the movie. BUT, if you see a movie where the creators had limited funds, and it sometimes seems they were more concerned with a time line for releasing their film, than quality of the film, you can see edits.

Just like you had to make your mistakes, so does your prodigal. Are you trying to make their edits? Whether a child, spouse, brother, sister, parent. It is so hard to watch!!!! And especially when it seems, they just are too old, "they should know better"! Right?! In those cases, I would like to edit certain parts of their "stories", so they will not have to get hurt or face yet another consequence of the choices they're making today. But I don't want their life to end up like a cheap movie. I don't want to see the awkward pauses either! I want it to be smooth and flawless!

So, what do we do next?

We pray, we wait, we (only when God leads) give them fair warning. BUT most of the time we are just there to watch. To witness the awkward pauses, to be there when their story takes yet another crazy turn, and they need someone to hold their hand. It's in those moments that you just do that, YOU JUST HOLD THEIR HAND! You don't offer unsolicited advice, you don't say "I told you so", you don't shame them (they already feel enough shame at this point, even if it doesn't seem that way). You just Love. That's it that's all, JUST LOVE! Jesus said "the greatest of these (faith, hope and love) is love". That's the greatest thing you can do.

> *"Above all, love each other deeply,*
> *because love covers over a multitude of sins."*
> ***I Peter 4:8*** *NIV*

Trust me, if you do only that (LOVE), it will surprise them! It will shrink the chasm between you, and it will avoid yet another unwanted argument. Do not be afraid that your silence means you agree. You can discuss that another day, and for those whose children have been raised in a Christian atmosphere and you know that you taught them correctly, THEY KNOW HOW YOU FEEL AND WHAT YOU BELIEVE! Our children, seemed to always remind us of that any time we questioned things. If you just continue to love, there will be a day when they return to you to tell you the rest of the story. To tell you how they saw God working, and felt His presence in times of need.

In the end GOD will make all the edits. He will make their story come to life with just the right edits. He's the King of edits! His BLOOD covers a multitude of sins! How about you and I just sit back and watch, and allow our Lord and Savior to make the film, and His name will be the only name when the credits roll. That's certainly ok with me!!

Thank God that He is The Editor
Let Him remind you how He has edited your life

Dear Lord,

I just want to ask You to help me today to trust in Your ability to edit the life of _____.

Thank You Jesus for making it possible that any of us have the advantage of Your editing! Give _____ _____ the ability to see Your hand in their life, and how great You are at editing. I choose today to rest in Your abilities and not depend on my own limited abilities. Help me to love as You do, without boundaries, or requirements. Thank You Lord for Your overwhelming Love!

In Jesus Name
AMEN

Suggested song: "Give Up" by Gaither Vocal Band (Southern Classics album)

LOVE ENDURES ALL THINGS

I know that most of you have probably had the same experiences as myself. I've read certain chapters of the Bible so many times and one day as you read the Lord highlights a portion for you and makes yet another thought clearer than ever before. Well that's exactly what happened to me a few weeks ago when I was doing my daily reading. I just love how the Lord brings scripture to life in our lives. That's why it is so important for us to study His word daily to "chew" on His word and to apply it to our lives.

When I was a younger Christian and a new pastor's wife, I felt guilty that I had not read the Bible all the way through. I was never a good reader, and I had a very difficult time comprehending or retaining anything that I read (which the Lord healed me of, but that story is for another day). However, a friend of ours came and spoke at our church, his name was Ron Auch (he has now gone to entertain the Lord in heaven). But he would say... "If reading through the Bible seems daunting to you, I want to encourage you that if you read one chapter a day, you can read the Bible through in three years' time."

Now I can do that!! And have done that ever since. I read no more than two chapters a day, most days, because this exercise taught me that I enjoy "chewing" on God's Word in small bites.

> *"Love is patient, love is kind. It does not envy,*
> *it does not boast, it is not proud.*
> *It does not dishonor others, it is not self-seeking,*
> *it is not easily angered,*
> *it keeps no record of wrongs.*
> *It always protects,*
> *always trusts, always hopes,*
> *always perseveres. Love never fails"*
> ***I Corinthians 13:4***

Those verses, right there, should be "chewed on" for days!

I Corinthians 13 is the love chapter and I've read it many, many times and most of us could probably quote it verbatim because we've heard it so often at weddings. But at the end of all of the "love is" portions is verse 7, speaking of Love, and it says "it endures all things". OH, that just hit me so hard!!! After everything that we've been through the Lord needs us to know that love endures ALL things. I want to say that again LOVE ENDURES ALL THINGS, PERIOD. This was such an encouragement and revelation to me that because of the love that we have through Christ (I remind you that it is HIS love in us that does all the things mentioned in I Corinthians 13) we have been able to endure all of these things because HIS LOVE gives us the strength that we need to carry on.

In Paul's letters to all the different churches there is a common thread that we can clearly see. HE HAS ENDURED! To his credit, and our encouragement, it can be done!

Today I want to encourage you to endure all things with God's love, with the love of the Father, the love of the Son, and the love of the Holy Spirit. Thank God that we can depend on Him, we can trust in Him, we can lean on Him fully and endure all things. HIS LOVE is complete, ours is not. What a wonderful legacy to leave in our wake, a person that loved AND endured.

When you have difficulties in your life when you have people in your life that cause frustrations and cause issues, and have left you with a remnant of life you never expected, you can love and you can endure. May the love of the Lord and His peace go with you everywhere that you step your foot today, and every other. BE FULLY COMPLETE IN HIM!

Have you ever caused someone in your life to "endure"? Think on that, this may change the way you see Your current circumstances

Dear Heavenly Father,

We praise You for who You are and how You encourage us. I asked today that You penetrate my heart with Your love, to not only be patient and kind, but also to endure all that is thrown before me. Thank You Lord, that whatever comes my way, first has to pass through You. It is so encouraging to know that if You have allowed this in my life, then You have a plan to use it to help me, and those around me, grow and be even more complete in You. Give me the strength I need today to continue on and to shine Your love in the process.

In Jesus Name
AMEN

Suggested song: "Fullness" by Elevation Worship (official lyric video)

DAY 25

OVERCOMER OR OVERCOME

When you've been in a battle for so long there comes a point in time, may be several times, that you just want to give up. I'm telling you my friend, that is not the time to give up! It is more than likely the time that the battle is at its most pivotal point. It seems like just when you think you're coming to an end of a battling season that the enemy comes from the other side and attacks once again. But we cannot choose to be overcome. Yes, it is a choice! We are weary "I just wanna lay down", we think, and we just don't want to fight anymore. I GET IT! But we cannot allow the enemy to lull us into that place of laying down. WE MUST OVERCOME, WE MUST BE THE OVERCOMER!

I am so thankful to the Lord for placing all kinds of praying women (and some of their spouses) around us! When David went out to battle, he did not go out alone, he went out with his mighty men. The Lord has placed in our lives a lot of mighty women and men, and I am so very thankful that they are there to watch our backs and hold up our arms when we need it. These men and women help us to get through the battle, help us to see the other side and help defeat the enemies in our lives.

Just recently we had a battle we needed to fight. All I had to do was put out a few texts and I knew that our battle was covered, I knew that we were going to go through this battle with others by our side locked arm-in-arm defeating the enemy in our lives and in our family's lives.

Prayer Warriors give us strength, and the more we have the more strength we have. Sometimes we are tempted to keep our "secrets" to ourselves, those things in our lives that we feel others don't necessarily need to know. Admitting that we or one of our family members has chosen a wrong path once again. Well, may I suggest you "break off" the spirit of pride in your life and ask for help?! Every seasoned warrior knows he needs an army to defeat an army. Unless the Lord is telling you to do this on your own, you need to enlist your battle tested friends to come along side of you. Sometimes we are just "too close" to see the full picture, and allowing others, who have done battle before, to maybe give us another perspective ALWAYS helps. I want to reiterate one thing though..."battle tested", that means they have been exposed to a battle or two, or more, before, and they know how to proceed. Also, be VERY careful who you "open up" to. There are those that can handle these secrets and there are those who should NEVER know a secret.

Years ago, I felt led that every Tuesday I was supposed to pray in the sanctuary of our church. I KNEW BEYOND A SHADOW OF A DOUBT that this was going to be a battle. So, I was strapping on my battling boots, when a "more seasoned" friend came to me and said "I need to do this with you". I agreed and the next week we were walking down the hall to begin our battle, when she said "oh we can't go in there without being covered ". She proceeded to pray a "covering" over our families and us. "WOW", I thought, "I never even considered that I needed that!" BUT I DID NEED THAT! And God placed my friend Joyce there to help and protect me.

We are actually going through a battle right now, and I have enlisted several friends to lift up this need. God has shown other people things, that He hasn't shown me. I am perfectly ok with that! As a matter of fact, I am grateful for that! In the process of this particular battle I have seen pictures of clouds in my mind's eye and of dragons. I don't take this as "you are too small and the enemy is so big", but as a reminder that I am still in the midst of battle and the enemy is raising his ugly head. WELL, THAT ENEMY IS GOING DOWN!!

Friends, don't give up!

> *"Let us not become weary in doing good,*
> *for at the proper time we will reap a harvest*
> ***if we do not give up."***
> **Galatians 6:9** *NIV*

> *"When Moses's hands grew tired...*
> *Aaron and Hur held his hands up-one on one side,*
> *one on the other-*
> *so that his hands remained steady till sunset."*
> **Exodus 17:12** *NIV*

Consider who your "battle tested" friends are
We need to know before any onslaught comes our way!

Dear Jesus,

Please give me all the strength, wisdom, and insight I need to be the overcomer of this battle. Thank You that You place others in our lives to come by our side and help us when we are in need. Please help me to be willing to share my battles with those You have placed in my path, but also please give me discernment about those that I should not mention these things to. Thank You for Your Spirit of Strength that You give us, to finish this battle! And help me never to grow so weary that I give up. Please cover all of us with Your blood and protection as we carry on this battle.

In Jesus Name
AMEN

Suggested song: "Fear No More" by Building 429

WHAT TIME IS IT?

Have you ever wondered about the time frame of things? At times I get so enamored with time. I just want to be "in the know" of Gods time frame. I desire to hear the conversations of the Godhead. I get so caught up with "time" that I lose time. I spend so much time thinking about time that time alludes me. CAN YOU SAY "HAMSTER WHEEL"?

This IS NOT the place I desire to be!!! I want to be "present" for every moment. I want to spend my time wisely. I want to use every moment to bring glory, honor and praise to my King in everything I say and do. I don't want to spend so much time on the "what if's" that I lose my focus on what is right now.

When you have a family member, or friend that just doesn't seem to let God do His work in their life, you can tend to take on the **self-induced** responsibility of listening for them, or trying to figure out what you can do to cause a change. NOW LISTEN TO THIS LOUD AND CLEAR.... STOP IT RIGHT NOW!!

In most cases (not all) giving your "tribe" to God daily is all that's required. Beyond that we need to get out of Gods way and let Him take control of their lives. Sometimes (most times) this just doesn't look the way we want it to and it is definitely not in the time frame we desire.

I have gotten so weary in the waiting! Honestly, I get over-whelmed in the waiting. BUT when I find myself in this place, I have to intentionally refocus on Who my God is, and on the fact that He loves them more than I. He has a plan and a time frame that I could never understand, and probably would not want to!

> *"For I know the plans I have for you," declares the Lord,"*
> *plans to prosper you and not to harm you,*
> *plans to give you hope and a future.*
> *Then you will call on Me and come and pray to Me,*
> *and I will listen to you.*
> *You will seek Me and find Me*
> *when you seek Me with all your heart.*
> *I will be found by you," declares the Lord,*
> *"and will bring you back from captivity.*
> *I will gather you from all the nations*
> *and places where I have banished you,"*
> *declares the Lord, "and will bring you back to the place*
> *from which I carried you into exile."*
> **Jeremiah 29:11**
> *(my emphasis added)*

Do you see who the Lord is speaking to there? He's speaking to those who have not found Him yet (not that those who have are excluded).

So, my dear friend, please do as I am trying to, and get off that hamster wheel, and get on to what God has placed before you. There are others in our lives that are also waiting, waiting for us to pay attention to them and their needs, instead of just being focused on that one needy, high maintenance person, that is responsible for delaying the entire process.

Gods timing is perfect! ALWAYS PERFECT! And we must learn to walk away and rest as we place every situation in His hands!

"There is a time for everything,
and a season for every activity under the heaven
a time to be born and a time to die,
a time to plant and a time to uproot,
a time to kill and a time to heal,
a time to tear down and a time to build,
a time to weep and a time to laugh,
a time to mourn and a time to dance,
a time to scatter stones and a time to gather them,
a time to embrace and a time to refrain from embracing,
a time to search and a time to give up,
a time to keep and a time to throw away,
a time to tear and a time to mend,
a time to be silent and a time to speak,
a time to love and a time to hate,
a time for war and a time for peace.
He has made everything beautiful in its time.
He has also set eternity in the human heart;
yet no one can fathom what God has done
from beginning to end".
Ecclesiastes 3:1

Who could you pay more attention to today?
Instead of focusing on the "prodigal" in your life

Dear Heavenly Father,

Thank You, that You are the God who sees us where we are, but also the God that sees what is ahead. I am so grateful today that You are my God and that I can trust in You to take _____ to the finish line of life. You remind us continually in Your Word that You are worthy to be trusted with everything. Help me today to place this mess in Your hands once again and trust that I don't need to have the answers for _____, You already have the answers and the next steps planned. I place _____ in Your hands again today.

In Jesus Name
AMEN

Suggested song: "Now Is The Time" by Evie Tornquist ***This is an oldie!! Enjoy!!

DAY 27

SACRIFICING YOUR DREAMS

What a whirlwind of emotion Abraham must have felt when the Lord asked him to sacrifice his only son!! Can you imagine? I hope I would never try to be so presumptuous as to put myself in ANYONES place, and assume I know how they feel or should respond.

If you would take time to read **Genesis 22** today, before you continue reading the rest of today's devotional, that would be a great.

To read these passages from **Genesis 22**, we do not get any inclination as to what Abraham was feeling or even thinking. All we know is that his first act was to obey and that he left early. We also read that it took him three days to get to the mountain God chose. What went through his mind during those three days? Maybe he started out by thinking "Am I hearing you right God? This is the son of promise, this is the son that all those dreams of mine were going to be fulfilled through, what am I doing?"

I believe that there's a possibility that The Lord used those three days it took to get to that mountain to prepare Abraham's heart, that possibly He used that time to remind Abraham how He has led him through all these years, that He has been faithful to fulfill the promises He had given Abraham.

That this is yet another opportunity for Him to show Abraham, and now Isaac, His mighty power and deliverance. So, by the end of that three-day journey, when Isaac asked where the lamb for the burnt offering was, Abraham was very confident in saying "God Himself will provide the lamb for the burnt offering my son."

Today my husband and I face a similar test. "Place your children and all your dreams attached to them on the altar of sacrifice (not quite the same though, Abrahams was a real alter, our is figurative) and give it all to me," WOW! I thought we had done that already! But yet once again we are challenged to climb that mountain and give them up.

I think, for us, this has come in stages. There are different "dreams" attached each time we take these precious sacrifices to The Lord, that we must now give over. This ends up being a sacrifice of thanksgiving and praise because WE SERVE JEHOVAH-JIREH, THE LORD OUR PROVIDER!!

Now we know that Jesus is the ultimate replacement! But today is about the process! When we continue to try to step in and make these children what we want to see them be, God comes along and says "give them to me, let Me make them what I always intended". So, what do we do? Do we fight GOD ALMIGHTY? OF COURSE NOT!! We remind ourselves, or allow God to remind us, since we so easily forget, of all the times in the past that Our God Has Been Faithful to Perform His Marvelous Acts of Loving Kindness! We put those lambs on Gods altar and we let Him provide the ultimate replacement!

This is not only a testimony to us but to our children as well!

Take time to write out
Your loved one(s) name(s)
Then write out all your dreams
(Whatever you have wished for them, or Dreamed they
would do or be
OR even what dreams would come
True for you through them)
That you have attached to them
Then lay it down before you, as on an altar
Then pray todays prayer

Lord God, Heavenly Father,

I come to You today with Praise and thanksgiving for all You have done. For all Your mighty acts, and all Your tender mercies that are new every morning. Thank You for reminding me of all that You have done in the past, and that You are ALWAYS able to complete what You have begun. Thank You for Your patience with me, thank You that the sacrifices I bring to You today, I can trust You with. I leave these sacrifices on Your altar today and I expect You to perform miracles to provide their replacement. Thank You that I can trust You and that I can be at peace with this sacrifice. Thank You Jesus! for You are the ultimate replacement and sacrifice in all of this!

In Jesus Name
AMEN

NOW DESTROY THAT PAPER!
It's all in God's hands now!
Suggested song: "Blessed Be Your Name" by Newsong

DAY 28

JOY COMES IN THE MORNING

After such a "heavy" day yesterday, we must be reminded that "Joy comes in the morning"

> *"For His anger lasts only a moment,*
> *but His favor lasts a lifetime;*
> *weeping may stay for the night,*
> *but rejoicing comes in the morning."*
> **Psalms 30:5** NIV
> *(my emphasis added)*

We must continually remember that all these things we are facing ARE TEMPORARY, let me shout that again...THIS MESS IS TEMPORARY!!!!

When you find yourselves mourning over the disappointments of life, please let me remind you that joy comes in the morning, not in the mourning!

There is a time for everything just as it says in Ecclesiastes, but once you have mourned, get yourself back into the place of receiving joy.

I can't remember who I was listening to today on line (my husband and I spent many hours today listening to others leading us in worship, it may have been CC Winans), but they were talking about who God is and that's where our joy comes from. So, let's elaborate for a moment...

He's The Great I AM

He's Jehovah-Jireh (Provider)

He's Jehovah-Rapha(Healer)

He's our best friend

He's our Strength

He's Faithful

He's The Truth

He's The Life

He's The Bright Morning Star

He's The God who spoke EVERYTHING into existence

He's The Alpha and The Omega

He's Wisdom

He's The Prince of Peace

He's The Wonderful Counselor

He's The Mighty God

He's Love

He's our Strong Tower

He's Jehovah El Roi (The God who sees)

His Mercies are new every morning

And I could go on and on and on!! You can listen to Aaron Jeoffrey! They have a great song about who God is from Genesis to Revelation.

The point here is we have to refocus, we have to choose to leave all this stuff in God's hands, and remember Whom we serve, and Who is ultimately in control (because we give it over to Him). Don't allow the enemy to steal another moment of joy from you! Call his bluff! You know that is what that little mite does, he tries to make you feel like all this mess is your fault. he even tries to tell you that you are not covering this mess enough in prayer. REALLY? DON'T LET him CALL YOUR BLUFF, YOU CALL his!! You shout back "MY GOD'S GOT THIS!"

Pause and think about who God is to you

Heavenly Father,

I thank You today for my times with You. I thank You that You are all in all! I thank You that You are everything mentioned today, and that I can lay this mess in Your hands. And that in Your hands this mess is as small as a grain of sand. Thank You for this mess, because in it and through it I, and all those around me, will see Your intervention and Your miracles! Because You work all things together for us!!

In Jesus Name
AMEN

Suggested song: "He Is" by Aaron Jeoffrey (with lyrics)

OH, FOOLISH SOUL

Today I found myself not wanting to get out of bed. I found myself wallowing in my concern for my children and not seeing a good end in sight. I found myself saying "what is there to get up for?" "I will just sleep and forget all if this!!"

At the same time, I had a phrase (from a song) ringing in my thoughts "beruka haba b'shem Adonai". I couldn't remember what it meant; it was one of those annoying things that would not leave me alone! It caused me to crawl out of bed and look up what exactly it meant. I proceeded to my prayer room, sat in my prayer chair and pulled out my phone and began to type the words... ugh how do you spell that?? Well, I fumbled my way through and found that it means "Blessed is he who comes in the name of the Lord". Well that's nice, ok moving on, now at least I know.

I had no clue that God was trying to speak with me!! I was so enthralled with my moaning that I missed my cue from the Lord. Well, thank God He does not give up easily!! I proceeded to look up the bible study that I've been doing on line. Then I could hear God speaking a bit louder. It was a verse the Lord had spoken to me about in the past, I EVEN SPOKE ON IT BEFORE!! Here's what it said

> *"Bless the Lord, O my soul, and all that is within me,*
> *bless His Holy name!*
> *Bless the Lord, O my soul, and forget not all His benefits,"*
> **Psalms 103:1**
> (my emphasis added)

OH MY!!! HOW COULD I FORGET??!!

May I suggest you read the rest of Psalms 103? SOOO GOOD!!!

This scripture shows us how David, the man after Gods own heart, kept his heart in that place. How he kept himself in a place where God could claim that he was a man after Gods own heart. This is how, it's all right there!!! You force your soul (which is our will, feelings, emotions) to bless the Lord, even when you don't feel like it. You remind yourself with Gods Holy Scripture of all the wonderful attributes of our God! This allows us to regain our "footing" again, reestablishing ourselves in our firm foundation...The Christ Whom we serve!! Wow! Thank you Holy Spirit, for being so patient with me!

Well, He wasn't done! Remember the phrase that got me out of bed in the first place? "beruka haba b'shem Adonai", He brought me back to this, while writing this actually. He reminded me... BLESSED are you when you come! When you come seeking me, when you come with your questions, when you come with your concerns, when you come to me in my name, you are blessed! HALLELUJAH!! I SAY IT AGAIN ... HALLELUJAH!!! FOR THE LORD OUR GOD THE ALMIGHTY REIGNS! He reigns over all these seemingly STUPID circumstances, He reigns over my wallowing, He reigns over my expectations. Give thanks to the Lord for He is good; His love endures forever!!

So, if you find yourself in a similar state of mind, I want to encourage you to say to your soul " Bless the Lord" you foolish thing! Move over! I, with Gods help, am in charge of you, IT IS

NOT THE OTHER WAY AROUND! I will cause my soul to bow down, so my Spirit can rise up and shout!!

Pause and tell your soul "Bless The Lord oh my soul"!

Father,

Thank You for Your mercies that are new every morning! Thank You for loving us when we are unlovable. Thank You that You reach to us when we are unaware, and cause us to become aware! LORD, I LOVE YOU! I PRAISE YOU! I GLORIFY YOUR HOLY AND EXALTED NAME!! YOU ALONE ARE GOOD!! Thank You for reestablishing my footing today! Help me to remember this precept of Yours forever!

In Jesus Name
AMEN

Suggested song: "Roar from Zion" by Paul Wilbur (Live)

Two Bonus songs: "10,000 Reasons" (Bless The Lord) by Matt Redman

"Make Room" by Jonathan McReynolds

WITHHOLDING NOTHING

A re you "hooked" on any game shows? We seem to go thru seasons of watching, then seasons of not watching. It really depends on our schedule I suppose. This year we have been in the midst of a major transition, and found ourselves in a place where "Jeopardy" and "Wheel of Fortune" were our greatest form of entertainment for each day. (That's hard to admit, because I am not that old!!! We just had a lot of time on our hands for a few months.)

ANYWAY, last season we watched "Jeopardy James" take the game by storm. He was just amazing and his approach to the game was much different than anyone before him. You see the difference between him and the others that came before him (or after) is that he is a professional gambler. That makes a huge difference in the game, besides the fact that he is a person that is able to retain ENORMOUS amounts of information.

James did things others only wished they had the courage to do, he would go "ALL IN" on most every "Daily Double" question. As he would announce his "ALL IN" choice he would also make a motion with his hands like he was pushing poker chips to the center of a table.

It was amazing to watch him; we didn't want to miss a program because he was fun to watch and would totally blow most opponents away.

Well now I know you're asking "Krisan, what does this have to do with anything?"... I promise, I do have a point here!!!

You see, my husband and I were worshipping the Lord together in our home a few days ago, and my husband had just walked out of the room, as I sat there resting in the Fathers embrace, a song began to play. A voice seemed to come out of such a quiet peaceful place singing " I surrender all to you, everything I give to you, withholding nothing", it hit me so hard, I began to weep, I just wanted the Lord to know I would give Him anything. I found myself making the same gesture that James made on Jeopardy, "all in" Lord, I was picturing myself gathering up my children and grandchildren, and pushing them into God's presence.

What was obvious about James was that he was VERY confident in his ability. He had been in a gambling position before, so it did not give him pause, he was ready to take the chance to cause his "bank" to grow.

In my special moment with ABBA, I also like James found myself very confident. Not in my abilities, but in Abbas. I have been here before! I knew I could trust ABBA to take my "bank" and multiply it much better than I could. I knew that leaving my babies at His feet would bring me more peace than I would have if I didn't. Abba never asks us to do anything He hasn't already done.

> *"For God so loved the world*
> *that He gave His one and only Son,*
> *that whoever believes in Him shall not perish*
> *but have eternal life."*
> **John 3:16** NIV
> *(my emphasis added)*

God was "all in" before we were even a thought to our parents! He was "all in" before time began and He will be "all in" when this world we know of ceases to exist. He is Alpha and Omega, beginning and End.

HE IS ALL IN ALL!!!

Are you willing to trust Abba with your precious "bank"
That you've been investing in for years?
Are you "all in"?

Dearest ABBA,

Thank You for the privilege of investing into
_____ life. Thank You
for the blessings that You have brought to me
through them. Thank You that You have given
me grace and strength to go through this process
and to walk this journey. I will forever be grateful
to You for the strength and peace You bring to
me on a regular basis. Help me to be "ALL IN"
now, help me to trust You and Your faithfulness
with _____.
In Jesus Name
AMEN

Suggested song: "Withholding Nothing Medley" by William
McDowell from album Withholding Nothing

DAY 31

DELIVERED BY
YOUR HANDS

A s my final daily journal for this book I want to
share the encouragements that the Lord has given
me over these years. I want them to be an encouragement to you as they were to me.

I don't know if you have ever had the wonderful experience of hearing God speak to you, or being in a conference where others speak "prophetic words" over
another. It is an awesome experience that at first, if
you're hearing it for another person, can make you
feel like you are being left out, BUT THAT IS NOT THE
CASE AT ALL! You see, when God gives "words" to
others, a lot of the time (not always) those "words", we
can claim for ourselves as well. Furthermore, I believe,
even if you think you have never heard God's voice,
you probably have. Just listen carefully, and give yourself time after praying to listen. Recently, I heard one
wise lady say "You should be giving the Lord at least a
half hour to speak to you after you have prayed". Oooh,
well, let's at least try!!

So, I want to encourage you to claim anything that I
share as "a word that God gave me" or anything that
has been inspired of God in this book, as your own. You
claim it for you and yours. You decree and declare it
over your own.

"You will also declare a thing,
And it will be established for you;
So light will shine on your ways.
When they cast you down,
and you say, 'Exaltation will come!'
Then He will save the humble person.
He will even deliver one who is not innocent;
Yes, He will be delivered by the purity of your hands."
Job 22:28
(my emphasis added)

Did you see that? *"Yes, he will be delivered by the purity of your hands"* WOOHOO...GO GOD!!!! Well, there's one! Ha, God is so good!! Here are some others...

"God is in control, and if we submit to Him, He will cause the victory to happen!"

"Sometimes God gives us a blessing, then asks us to give it back"...

So, "I'm giving them back and awaiting on a 'Better Return.'"

"When you entertain a thought from the enemy, then he comes in with another, then another...PUT ON THE HELMET OF SALVATION!"

"Do Not grow weary, Do Not faint! I AM the Lord Who strengthens thee! I AM, I AM, I AM, I AM, and you are the child who trusts in Me forevermore!!"

"My name is great and greatly to be praised! Do Not fear for I AM with you Do Not be afraid for I will steady you. I AM the hand you do not see; I AM the calm in the storm. DO NOT BE AFRAID!!"

*"The Lord is a refuge for the oppressed,
a stronghold in times of trouble.
Those who know Your name trust in You,
for You, Lord, have never forsaken those who seek You."*
Psalms 9:9
(my emphasis added)

*"Shout for joy, you heavens; rejoice, you earth;
burst into song, you mountains!
For the Lord comforts His people
and will have compassion on His afflicted ones."*
Isaiah 49:13 NIV
(my emphasis added)

*"The Lord himself goes before you and will be with you;
He will never leave you nor forsake you. Do not be afraid;
do not be discouraged."*
Deuteronomy 31:8 NIV
(my emphasis added)

*"The Lord your God has given you this land
to take possession of it."*
Deuteronomy 3:18a NIV

*"Therefore encourage one another and build each other up,
just as in fact you are doing."*
1 Thessalonians 5:11 NIV

My friends, the Lord wants you to be encouraged, He wants you to be victorious and He wants your precious "loved ones" to be victorious and successful as well. HE LOVES THEM MORE THAN YOU!!!

"The Lord bless you and keep you;
The Lord make His face shine upon you, And be
gracious to you;
The Lord lift up His countenance upon you, And give
you peace."
Numbers 6:24

Listen to "The Blessing" by Kari Jobe

Abba,

I Thank You so much for these friends that joined me on this month-long journey! I ask that You would bless them, and heal every wound of their soul. I thank You that You are actively working in each of our lives. Would You please bring the verses that they have learned here, back to their memory when they need it? Help them to follow You each day with all their heart. May they grow closer to You than ever before, because they can leave everything in Your hands. Bless them Lord beyond measure.

In Jesus Name
AMEN!!!

Suggested song: "Don't Give Up" by Andrae' Crouch

I LOVE YOU FRIENDS!!
THANKS FOR SHARING THIS JOURNEY!!
I AM PRAYING FOR EACH ONE OF YOU!!!

Prayer of Repentance and Commitment

Dear Heavenly Father,

I am asking You today to forgive me of every sin I have committed, knowingly or unknowingly. Please cleanse me from all the filth I have allowed in my life and teach me Your ways Lord.

Thank You so much for sending Your one and only Son to die for me! I declare to You today that I believe You sent Jesus to this earth through a virgin birth. I believe Jesus walked this earth as an example of how we should live. I believe Jesus died on the cross, as a payment for my sin. And I believe He rose from the dead to bring us life eternally. I also believe You sent Holy Spirit to help us, to lead us and guide us, while Jesus now lives in Heaven. I Choose today to serve you with every part of my being! Please accept me into the Kingdom of God clean, pure and whole before You.

In Jesus Name
AMEN

Explanation of Bible Translations and Abbreviations Used:

NIV ~ New International Version (1978/Biblica)

KJV ~ King James Version (1611/King James of England)

ESV ~ English Standard Version (2008/Crossway Bibles)

NASB ~ New American Standard Bible (1971/Lockman Foundation)

NLT ~ New Living Translation (1996/Tyndale House Foundation)

NKJV ~ New King James Version (1982/Thomas Nelson)

BBE ~ Bible in Basic English (1949/Cambridge University Press)

ESVUK ~ English Standard Version Anglicized (2001/Harper Collins)

YLT ~ Youngs Literal Translation (1862/Robert Young)

Referenced

Day 19 uses the definition of "Cypress" from Public domain and "Myrtle" from American Tract Society Bible Dictionary

Day 21 uses notes from One New Man Bible, True Potential Publishing

ABOUT THE AUTHOR

Krisan Markese has been in full time ministry for nearly 40 years, ministering with her husband Pastor Ron Markese. Krisan was ordained thru Joan Hunter Ministries in 2014 and has recently been serving in her local church in southwest Florida. She is also and more importantly mother to Stephanie and Mychal and "Nani" to Aiden and Ryan. Krisan has served in many different capacities over her years of ministry including music, supervising missions' trips, working with children, teens, young adults and adult ministries of all ages. Her passion is to draw others closer to our heavenly Father and give them insight as to how they relate to Him and He relates to them.

CPSIA information can be obtained
at www.ICGtesting.com
Printed in the USA
LVHW052341261120
672646LV00005B/478